BLUE CHEESE ASPARAGUS TUILES

Fresh parmesan cheese must be used in this recipe.

250g asparagus
1¼ cups (100g) finely grated parmesan cheese
¼ cup (30g) finely grated tasty cheddar cheese
2 tablespoons plain flour
⅓ cup (40g) chopped walnuts, toasted
fresh small sage leaves

FILLING
125g blue vein cheese, chopped
½ cup (125g) mascarpone cheese
2 teaspoons chopped fresh sage

Snap off coarse ends of asparagus spears. You will need to cut asparagus into 30 equal-sized pieces. Boil, steam or microwave asparagus until just tender, drain, rinse under cold water; drain well. Process cheeses and flour until mixture resembles fine breadcrumbs. Place a 5.5cm round cutter on baking paper-covered oven tray, fill evenly with 1½ teaspoons of cheese mixture, carefully remove cutter. Repeat with remaining cheese mixture, allowing 8 rounds per tray. Bake rounds in moderate oven about 5 minutes or until lightly browned. Slide metal spatula under each tuile, then quickly shape over handle of whisk or other utensil measuring about 3cm in diameter; leave until firm. Spoon filling into tuiles, sprinkle with nuts; top with asparagus and sage leaves.

Filling: Process blue vein cheese until just smooth, gently stir in mascarpone cheese and sage.

Makes about 30.

■ Tuiles and filling can be made 3 days ahead.
■ Storage: Tuiles, in airtight container. Filling, covered, in refrigerator.
■ Freeze: Not suitable.
■ Microwave: Not suitable.

SMOKED SALMON ROLLS

⅔ cup (100g) plain flour
2 eggs, lightly beaten
2 teaspoons vegetable oil
¾ cup (180ml) milk
1 tablespoon chopped fresh parsley
250g sliced smoked salmon
1 bunch fresh chives

CHEESE FILLING
125g packet cream cheese
1 tablespoon lemon juice
1 teaspoon Dijon mustard
1 teaspoon chopped fresh dil!

Sift flour into medium bowl, whisk in combined eggs, oil, milk and parsley. Pour ¼ cup (60ml) batter into greased 20cm crepe pan, cook until lightly browned underneath. Turn crepe, cook until browned on other side. Repeat with remaining batter. You will need 5 crepes for this recipe.

Spread crepes with cheese filling. Roll slices of salmon up tightly; place along

EDITOR: Maryanne Blacker

FOOD EDITOR: Pamela Clark

▪ ▪ ▪

DESIGNER: Kathleen Hunter

ARTISTS: Annemarlene Hissink, Verna McGeachin

▪ ▪ ▪

ASSISTANT FOOD EDITOR: Louise Patniotis

ASSOCIATE FOOD EDITOR: Enid Morrison

SENIOR HOME ECONOMISTS:
Kathy McGarry, Sophia Young

HOME ECONOMISTS: Angela Bresnahan, Annette Brien,
Janene Brooks, Karen Buckley, Justin Kerr, Nila Surjan,
Jodie Tilse, Lovoni Welch

EDITORIAL COORDINATOR: Elizabeth Hooper

KITCHEN ASSISTANT: Amy Wong

▪ ▪ ▪

STYLISTS: Marie-Helene Clauzon, Carolyn Fienberg,
Jane Hann, Cherise Koch

PHOTOGRAPHERS: Kevin Brown, Robert Clark,
Robert Taylor, Jon Waddy

▪ ▪ ▪

HOME LIBRARY STAFF:

ART DIRECTOR: Sue de Guingand

ASSISTANT EDITORS: Bridget Green, Lynne Testoni

EDITORIAL COORDINATOR: Fiona Lambrou

▪ ▪ ▪

ACP PUBLISHER: Richard Walsh

ACP DEPUTY PUBLISHER: Nick Chan

ACP CIRCULATION & MARKETING DIRECTOR:
Judy Kiernan

▪ ▪ ▪

Produced by The Australian Women's Weekly Home Library.
Cover separations by ACP Colour Graphics Pty Ltd., Sydney.
Colour separations by Network Graphics Pty. Ltd., Sydney.
Printing by Hannanprint, Sydney.
Published by ACP Publishing Pty. Limited,
54 Park Street, Sydney.
◆ AUSTRALIA: Distributed by Network Distribution
Company, 54 Park Street Sydney, (02) 282 8777.
◆ UNITED KINGDOM: Distributed in the U.K. by Australian
Consolidated Press (UK) Ltd, 20 Galowhill Rd, Brackmills,
Northampton NN4 7EE (01604) 760 456.
◆ CANADA: Distributed in Canada by Whitecap Books Ltd,
351 Lynn Ave, North Vancouver B.C. V7J 2C4 (604) 980 9852.
◆ NEW ZEALAND: Distributed in New Zealand by Netlink
Distribution Company, 17B Hargreaves St, Level 5,
College Hill, Auckland 1 (9) 302 7616.
◆ SOUTH AFRICA: Distributed in South Africa by Intermag,
PO Box 57394, Springfield 2137 (011) 493 3200.

▪ ▪ ▪

Finger Food No. 2

Includes index.
ISBN 1 86396 044 9

1. Cookery. 2. Snack Foods. (Series:
Australian Women's Weekly Home Library.)

641.53

▪ ▪ ▪

© A C P Publishing Pty. Limited 1995
ACN 053 273 546

▪ ▪ ▪

COVER: Clockwise from top left: Honey-Glazed Chicken
Wings, Thai Chicken Patties with Sweet Chilli Sauce, Crab
Rolls with Chilli Plum Sauce, page 60.
OPPOSITE: Spicy Tikka Prawns with Spinach Raita, page 70.
BACK COVER: Icy Chocolate Pecan Truffles, page 98.

▪ ▪ ▪

FINGER FOOD

No. 2

Planning a party with finger food is fun, and entertaining in
this style is as versatile and unstructured as the lifestyles of
today. It's especially good as guests mix and mingle so easily.
Whether formal or informal, the key to success is to plan
ahead. Decide how much food and drink to supply, depending
on the type of party. If it's a cocktail party, allow, say, 3 to 4
savouries per person. For an on-going party, allow up to 10 per
person. The order of hot and cold savouries is not important.
Then, for a fabulous finale, bring on our sweet sensations,
allowing 2 or 3 per person.

FOOD EDITOR

BRITISH & NORTH AMERICAN READERS: Please note that
Australian cup and spoon measurements are metric. A quick conversion
guide appears on page 127.
A glossary explaining unfamiliar terms and ingredients appears on page 122.

COLD SAVOURIES

Perfect for parties or any occasion, these delicious morsels will vanish in a bite or two! Some need to be cooked first, others are uncooked, many can be prepared ahead, while several are assembled just before serving; all are served cold. You'll love our 2-page specials where one basic idea is varied in many ways to include different toppings, fillings and flavours, for example, bruschetta, canapes, ribbon sandwiches, dips and dippers, and crunchy nutty nibbles.

SPINACH CREAM CHEESE ROLLS

1 bunch (500g) English spinach, chopped
60g butter
1/3 cup (50g) plain flour
3/4 cup (180ml) milk
3 eggs, separated
1/4 teaspoon ground nutmeg

FILLING
1 medium (200g) red pepper
100g packaged cream cheese, softened
pinch ground hot paprika
2 tablespoons chopped fresh chives

Line base and sides of 26cm x 32cm Swiss roll pan with baking paper.

Add spinach to pan of boiling water, drain immediately, rinse under cold water; drain. Finely chop spinach, squeeze with hands to remove liquid. You will need 1/2 cup (125g) finely chopped spinach for this recipe.

Melt butter in pan, add flour, stir over heat until bubbling. Remove from heat, gradually stir in milk, stir over heat until sauce boils and thickens; transfer to large bowl, cool 5 minutes. Stir in spinach, egg yolks and nutmeg. Beat egg whites in small bowl with electric mixer until soft peaks form; fold into spinach mixture in 2 batches. Pour mixture into prepared pan. Bake in moderately hot oven about 12 minutes or until firm. Turn onto wire rack covered with tea-towel, remove lining paper. Cut roll in half crossways, then lengthways to give 4 rectangles. Spread rectangles with filling, roll up from short sides, cover; refrigerate 1 hour. Cut rolls into 1cm rounds; top with reserved red pepper.

Filling: Quarter pepper, remove seeds and membranes. Grill pepper, skin side up, until skin blisters and blackens. Peel away skin, finely chop pepper. Reserve half the pepper. Combine remaining pepper with cheese, paprika and chives in bowl.

Makes about 32.

■ Recipe can be made a day ahead.
■ Storage: Covered, in refrigerator.
■ Freeze: Not suitable.
■ Microwave: Not suitable.

PARMESAN SHORTBREAD WITH GOATS' CHEESE TOPPING

1 cup (150g) plain flour
2 tablespoons self-raising flour
1 teaspoon ground cumin
1/4 teaspoon cayenne pepper
1 1/2 cups (120g) finely grated parmesan cheese
125g butter, chopped
1/4 cup (60ml) sour cream

GOATS' CHEESE TOPPING
1 small (150g) red pepper, roughly chopped
150g goats' cheese
125g packet cream cheese
1 tablespoon chopped fresh basil
1/4 cup (30g) chopped pecans, toasted

Process all ingredients until mixture forms a ball. Divide mixture in half, shape each half into a roll 4cm in diameter, cover; refrigerate 2 hours.

Cut rolls into 7mm rounds, place about 3cm apart on greased oven trays; refrigerate 30 minutes. Bake in moderate oven about 10 minutes or until browned; cool on trays.

Spoon goats' cheese topping into piping bag fitted with 5mm star tube, pipe mixture onto shortbreads, top with basil leaves, if desired.

Goats' Cheese Topping: Blend or process all ingredients until just combined, cover; refrigerate several hours.

Makes about 45.

■ Recipe can be made 3 days ahead.
■ Storage: Shortbread, in airtight container. Goats' cheese topping, covered, in refrigerator.
■ Freeze: Not suitable.
■ Microwave: Not suitable.

From top: Parmesan Shortbread with Goats' Cheese Topping; Spinach Cream Cheese Rolls.

Platter and tiles from Country Floors.

edge of crepes. Roll crepes firmly around salmon; trim ends. Cut each roll into 2cm pieces. Drop chives in pan of boiling water; rinse immediately under cold water. Tie each roll with a chive; trim ends.

Cheese Filling: Beat all ingredients together in small bowl with electric mixer until smooth.

Makes about 30.

■ Unsliced filled rolls can be made 2 days ahead.
■ Storage: Covered, in refrigerator.
■ Freeze: Crepes suitable.
■ Microwave: Not suitable.

BELOW: From back: Smoked Salmon Rolls; Blue Cheese Asparagus Tuiles.

China from Villeroy & Boch; tray, starfish and server from Morris Home & Garden Wares.

PRAWN AND CARAMELISED ONION PANCAKES

500g uncooked prawns
³/₄ cup (110g) plain flour
1 egg, lightly beaten
³/₄ cup (180ml) buttermilk
40g butter, melted
1 tablespoon chopped
**   fresh tarragon**
1 cup (250ml) sour cream
fresh coriander leaves

CARAMELISED ONION
50g butter
1 large (300g) red Spanish onion,
**   finely sliced**
2 tablespoons brown sugar
1 tablespoon balsamic vinegar
¹/₄ teaspoon ground black pepper
¹/₄ cup (60ml) water

Shell and devein prawns; finely chop. Sift flour into bowl; whisk in combined egg, buttermilk and butter until smooth. Stir in prawns and tarragon. Drop rounded teaspoons of mixture, in batches, into greased heavy-based pan, cook until bubbles appear, turn pancakes, cook until browned on other side; repeat with remaining mixture. Spoon sour cream onto pancakes; top with caramelised onion, then coriander.

Caramelised Onion: Melt butter in pan, add onion, cook, covered, over low heat 5 minutes. Add sugar, vinegar, pepper and water, stir over low heat about 15 minutes or until onion is very soft and mixture is thick and syrupy; cool.

Makes about 45.

■ Pancakes and caramelised onion can be made a day ahead.
■ Storage: Covered, separately, in refrigerator.
■ Freeze: Pancakes suitable.
■ Microwave: Not suitable.

ABOVE: Prawn and Caramelised Onion Pancakes.

Plate from Dinosaur Designs.

Dips, Salsa and Servers

Guacamole can be made 3 hours ahead, the corn salsa a day ahead, and the remaining dips 3 days ahead. All dips should be stored, covered, in refrigerator; none is suitable to freeze or microwave. Cheese and bacon chunks, Cajun pita crisps, mini roti and potato skins can be made a day ahead and stored in airtight containers. The first 3 servers, uncooked, can be frozen; none of the servers is suitable to microwave.

TOFU AND SEEDED MUSTARD DIP

We used Kikkoman firm tofu for this recipe.

297g packet tofu
3 green shallots, chopped
2 tablespoons plain yogurt
1 tablespoon cider vinegar
2 cloves garlic, chopped
2 teaspoons seeded mustard

Blend or process all ingredients until smooth, cover; refrigerate mixture 3 hours or overnight.
Makes about 2 cups (500ml).

GUACAMOLE

2 large (640g) avocados, chopped
3 cloves garlic, crushed
2 tablespoons lemon juice
1 teaspoon hot chilli sauce
1/3 cup (80ml) sour cream
1 medium (130g) tomato,
  seeded, chopped
1 small (100g) red Spanish onion,
  finely chopped

Blend or process avocados, garlic, juice, sauce and sour cream until smooth; stir in tomato and onion.
Makes about 3 cups (750ml).

ROASTED GARLIC AND SUN-DRIED TOMATO DIP

1 bulb (70g) garlic
cooking oil spray
3/4 cup sun-dried tomatoes in oil,
  drained, chopped
1/4 cup chopped fresh parsley
185g packaged cream cheese,
  chopped
1/4 cup (60ml) water

Place unpeeled garlic bulb on oven tray, coat with cooking oil spray. Bake, uncovered, in moderately hot oven about 45 minutes or until cloves are soft. Cool garlic 15 minutes, cut in half crossways, squeeze flesh from each garlic clove; blend or process flesh with remaining ingredients until smooth, cover; refrigerate 3 hours or overnight.
Makes about 1 1/2 cups (375ml).

EGGPLANT DIP

1 medium (300g) eggplant
1 cup (70g) stale breadcrumbs
2 cloves garlic, crushed
1/4 cup chopped fresh parsley
2 teaspoons ground cumin
1/2 teaspoon ground hot paprika
2 tablespoons lemon juice
1/4 cup (60ml) plain yogurt

Place eggplant on oven tray. Bake, uncovered, in moderate oven about 40 minutes or until soft. Place eggplant in plastic bag for 15 minutes. Remove eggplant skin; chop flesh. Blend or process eggplant with remaining ingredients until smooth, cover; refrigerate 3 hours or overnight.
Makes about 1 1/2 cups (375ml).

CORN SALSA

2 large (500g) tomatoes, seeded,
  finely chopped
130g can corn kernels, drained
1 tablespoon lime juice
1 tablespoon chopped fresh
  coriander leaves
1 small (100g) red Spanish onion,
  finely chopped
1 tablespoon olive oil
few drops Tabasco sauce

Combine all ingredients in bowl, cover; refrigerate 1 hour. Drain; discard liquid.
Makes about 2 cups (500ml).

MINI ROTI

These are good served warm or cold.

1 cup (50g) plain flour
2 green shallots, finely chopped
3/4 cup (180ml) boiling water,
  approximately

Sift flour into bowl, add shallots, quickly stir in enough boiling water to mix to a soft dough. Turn dough onto floured surface, knead until smooth. Roll rounded teaspoons of dough into balls, roll out to 6cm rounds. Cook rounds in batches, in lightly greased heavy-based pan, over low heat until browned on both sides; flatten roti with eggslice during cooking.
Makes about 30.

CHEESE AND BACON CHUNKS

1/2 cup (75g) plain flour
1 1/2 cups (225g) self-raising flour
90g butter, chopped
1/2 cup (40g) finely grated
  parmesan cheese
1/4 cup (60ml) tomato paste
3 bacon rashers, finely chopped
1 egg yolk
1 tablespoon water, approximately

Sift flours into large bowl, rub in butter. Stir in cheese, paste, bacon, egg yolk and enough water to mix to a soft dough. Knead dough gently on lightly floured surface until smooth.

Divide dough into 3 portions, roll each portion between sheets of baking paper to 27cm x 32cm rectangle. Place each rectangle onto greased oven tray. Bake

in moderately hot oven about 15 minutes or until browned. Turn rectangles over, bake further 5 minutes or until browned. Cool on wire racks; break into pieces.

CAJUN PITA CRISPS

5 large pita pocket breads
1/4 cup (60ml) olive oil
1 tablespoon Cajun seasoning

Split each pita bread in half, cut each half into quarters. Place bread in single layer on oven trays. Brush with oil; sprinkle with seasoning. Bake in moderately hot oven about 10 minutes or until browned and crisp.
Makes 40.

POTATO SKINS

Potato skins can be served hot or cold.

8 medium (1.6kg) old potatoes
2 tablespoons olive oil
1 tablespoon chopped fresh rosemary
2 teaspoons salt
1 teaspoon cracked black pepper

Place unpeeled potatoes on oven tray; bake, uncovered, in moderate oven about 1 hour or until tender; cool. Cut each potato into 6 wedges, scoop out flesh, leaving skins intact; reserve potato flesh for another use.

Place potato skins in single layer on wire rack over oven tray. Brush with oil, sprinkle with combined rosemary, salt and pepper. Bake, uncovered, in hot oven about 20 minutes or until crisp.
Makes 48.

1. Roasted Garlic and Sun-Dried Tomato Dip **2.** Tofu and Seeded Mustard Dip **3.** Eggplant Dip **4.** Guacamole **5.** Corn Salsa **6.** Mini Roti **7.** Cheese and Bacon Chunks **8.** Potato Skins **9.** Cajun Pita Crisps.

Setting from Corso De' Fiori; tiles from Country Floors.

7

CHEESE AND HERB PINWHEELS

1 teaspoon oil
3 bacon rashers, chopped
6 green shallots, chopped
375g packaged cream cheese,
  softened
1 tablespoon chopped
  fresh rosemary
1/4 cup chopped fresh chives
1 tablespoon chopped fresh basil
1/2 cup (40g) flaked almonds, toasted
250g packet pumpernickel rounds
chopped fresh chives, extra

Heat oil in pan, add bacon and shallots, cook, stirring, until bacon is crisp; cool.

Blend or process bacon mixture, cheese and herbs until smooth. Spread mixture onto sheet of foil to 25cm x 28cm rectangle, place on tray, cover; refrigerate 30 minutes. Sprinkle almonds over cheese mixture, roll up cheese mixture firmly from long side, using foil as a guide, cover; refrigerate 1 hour or until firm. Cut roll into 1cm slices, place on pumpernickel rounds; top with extra chives.
Makes about 30.

■ Cheese mixture can be made
  3 days ahead.
■ Storage: Covered, in refrigerator.
■ Freeze: Not suitable.
■ Microwave: Bacon mixture suitable.

PUMPERNICKEL SALMON ROUNDS

3/4 cup (180ml) sour cream
2 tablespoons chopped fresh dill
250g packet pumpernickel rounds
10 slices (200g) smoked salmon,
  sliced
fresh dill sprigs, extra
tiny lemon wedges, peeled, halved

Combine cream and dill in bowl; spoon onto pumpernickel rounds. Top with salmon, extra dill and lemon.
Makes about 30.

■ Recipe can be made 3 hours ahead.
■ Storage: Covered, in refrigerator.
■ Freeze: Not suitable.

GRAVLAX ON DILL PIKELETS

1/2 cup (75g) self-raising flour
1 egg yolk
1/2 cup (125ml) milk
1 1/2 tablespoons chopped
  fresh dill
80g sliced gravlax, chopped
fresh dill sprigs, extra

TOPPING
2/3 cup (170g) mascarpone cheese
2 teaspoons seeded mustard

Sift flour into bowl, gradually wi[...] combined egg yolk, milk and dill; [...] until smooth. Drop teaspoons of m[...] into heated greased heavy-based pan, cook until bubbles appear, turn pikelets, brown on other side; cool on wire rack. Spoon topping into piping bag fitted with 7mm plain tube. Pipe topping onto pikelets, top with gravlax and extra dill.
Topping: Combine cheese and mustard in bowl, mix well.
Makes about 40.

■ Recipe can be made several
  hours ahead.
■ Storage: Covered, in refrigerator.
■ Freeze: Pikelets suitable.
■ Microwave: Not suitable.

LEFT: From top: Pumpernickel Salmon Rounds; Cheese and Herb Pinwheels. BELOW: Gravlax on Dill Pikelets.

Left: Setting from Orson & Blake Collectables.

Ribbon Sandwiches

These 10 recipes have one thing in common: each has a slice of bread "sandwiched" in the middle that has a spread on both sides to help the sandwich keep its shape when cut into thirds. Butter is used for this purpose in 5 of the recipes, while the other half use similarly creamy spreads, such as mayonnaise, yogurt or horseradish cream. Each recipe uses 30 pieces of bread, 3 slices in each of 10 sandwiches, crusts removed and cut into a trio of fingers. Use whatever kind of bread you prefer; we used white and wholemeal. Each recipe makes 30 ribbon sandwiches; all can be made a few hours ahead of serving and kept, covered, in the refrigerator. None of these recipes is suitable to freeze or microwave.

KUMARA AND BLUE CHEESE

1 large (500g) kumara, thinly sliced
cooking oil spray
1/2 cup (125ml) mango chutney
60g butter, softened
300g blue vein cheese
2/3 cup (80g) chopped walnuts
1/4 cup (60ml) milk
1/3 cup chopped fresh basil

Heat greased griddle pan; coat kumara with cooking oil spray, cook in batches until browned on both sides and tender. Spread 10 bread slices with chutney, top with a single layer of kumara. Spread another 10 slices with butter; place, butter side down, over kumara. Top with combined cheese, walnuts, milk and basil, then remaining 10 bread slices.

PROSCIUTTO, BEAN AND SPINACH

40g butter
2 x 310g cans butter beans,
**   rinsed, drained**
8 green shallots, finely chopped
2 cloves garlic, crushed
1 1/2 tablespoons chopped
**   fresh thyme**
1 tablespoon chopped
**   fresh rosemary**
3/4 cup (180ml) chicken stock
10 slices (150g) prosciutto
125g butter, softened, extra
10 large (80g) English
**   spinach leaves**

Heat butter in pan, add beans, shallots, garlic and herbs, cook, stirring, until shallots are soft. Add stock, simmer, uncovered, until beans are almost pulpy; cool 10 minutes. Spread warm bean mixture equally over 20 slices of bread; top 10 of these with a single layer of prosciutto. Spread remaining 10 slices with extra butter on both sides, place over prosciutto. Top with spinach, then remaining bean mixture slices.

TURKEY, MINT AND CHERRY

425g can stoneless black cherries
**   in syrup**
2 teaspoons vegetable oil
1 clove garlic, crushed
1 1/2 teaspoons dry mustard
1 1/2 tablespoons cornflour
1/4 cup (60ml) water
3 cups (500g) finely chopped
**   cooked turkey**
300g carton sour cream
1/3 cup chopped fresh mint
125g butter, softened

Drain cherries, reserve syrup; chop cherries. Heat oil in small pan, add garlic and mustard, cook, stirring, until fragrant, stir in cherries and syrup. Add blended cornflour and water, stir over heat until mixture boils, simmer, uncovered, until mixture is reduced to 1 cup (250ml); cool. Combine turkey, cream and mint in bowl, spread equally over 10 slices of bread; spread cherry mixture over another 10 slices of bread. Spread remaining 10 slices with butter on both sides; sandwich each between the turkey and cherry slices.

SMOKED SALMON AND CAPER

2 x 250g tubs soft cream cheese
1/4 cup (60g) drained capers, chopped
2 tablespoons finely
**   chopped gherkins**
1/3 cup chopped fresh parsley
500g sliced smoked salmon
125g butter, softened

Combine half the cheese with capers and gherkins in bowl. Combine remaining cheese with parsley in separate bowl. Spread 10 slices of bread with caper mixture and another 10 slices with parsley mixture. Top all 20 with the salmon. Spread remaining 10 slices with butter on both sides; sandwich each between the 2 other slices.

CHICKEN AND TAHINI

5 cups (850g) finely chopped
**   cooked chicken**
1 3/4 cups (430ml) plain yogurt
3/4 cup chopped fresh
**   coriander leaves**
1/3 cup (80ml) tahini
1/4 cup (60ml) lemon juice
2 teaspoons ground cumin
2 teaspoons sambal oelek
2/3 cup (50g) flaked almonds, toasted
1/2 cup (125ml) plain yogurt, extra
1 medium (170g) green cucumber,
**   thinly sliced**

Combine chicken with yogurt, coriander, tahini, juice, cumin and sambal oelek in bowl. Spread chicken mixture equally over 20 slices of bread; top 10 with equal amounts of almonds, then a bread slice spread on both sides with extra yogurt. Place cucumber over yogurt; cover with remaining 10 chicken mixture slices.

Combine butter and curry powder in small pan, cook, stirring, until fragrant. Combine curry mixture, eggs, coconut cream and coriander in bowl, cover; refrigerate 1 hour. Spread egg mixture equally over 20 slices of bread. Spread remaining 10 slices with extra butter on both sides; sandwich each between the 2 egg mixture slices.

GRILLED PEPPER, FETA AND OLIVE PASTE

4 large (1.4kg) red peppers
600g feta cheese
1 cup (250ml) olive paste
125g butter, softened

Quarter peppers, remove seeds and membranes. Grill peppers, skin side up, until skin blisters and blackens. Peel away skin. Cut cheese into 7mm slices, grill on 1 side until browned. Divide olive paste equally over 20 slices of bread. Top 10 using all the cheese; top other 10 slices using all the peppers. Spread remaining 10 slices with butter on both sides; sandwich each between the cheese and pepper slices.

BACON, PINE NUT AND CHILLI SAUCE

15 bacon rashers, finely chopped
3/4 cup (180ml) mild sweet chilli sauce
1 1/4 cups (40g) shredded butter lettuce
1 cup (250ml) mayonnaise
3/4 cup (120g) pine nuts, toasted

Add bacon to pan, cook, stirring, until browned and crisp; drain. Spread chilli sauce equally over 20 slices of bread; top 10 of these with lettuce, half the bacon and half the pine nuts. Spread remaining 10 slices with mayonnaise on both sides; place over pine nuts. Top with remaining bacon and pine nuts; cover with remaining 10 chilli sauce slices.

PESTO AND TOMATO

1 cup firmly packed basil leaves
1/3 cup (50g) pine nuts, toasted
1/4 cup (20g) finely grated parmesan cheese
1 clove garlic, crushed
1/4 cup (60ml) olive oil
300g bocconcini cheese, thinly sliced
6 medium (450g) egg tomatoes, thinly sliced
3/4 cup (180ml) mayonnaise

Process basil, pine nuts, parmesan and garlic until smooth. Add oil in a thin stream while motor is operating; process pesto until combined. Divide pesto equally among 20 slices of bread; top 10 with bocconcini and 10 with tomatoes. Spread remaining 10 slices with mayonnaise on both sides; sandwich each between the bocconcini and tomato slices.

ROAST BEEF AND HORSERADISH

400g quark cheese
1/3 cup chopped fresh dill
500g sliced rare roast beef
1/3 cup (80ml) horseradish cream

Combine cheese and dill in bowl, spread equally over 20 slices of bread; top each with roast beef. Spread remaining 10 slices with horseradish cream on both sides; sandwich each between the 2 cheese and beef slices.

COCONUT AND CURRIED EGG

20g butter
3 teaspoons mild curry powder
12 hard-boiled eggs, finely chopped
1/2 cup (125ml) coconut cream
1/3 cup chopped fresh coriander leaves
125g butter, softened, extra

1. Chicken and Tahini 2. Coconut and Curried Egg 3. Kumara and Blue Cheese 4. Prosciutto, Bean and Spinach 5. Turkey, Mint and Cherry 6. Smoked Salmon and Caper 7. Roast Beef and Horseradish 8. Pesto and Tomato 9. Grilled Pepper, Feta and Olive Paste 10. Bacon, Pine Nut and Chilli Sauce.

SEAFOOD MOUSSE IN PASTRY CASES

1½ cups (225g) plain flour
125g butter, chopped
2 tablespoons chopped fresh dill
1 egg yolk
2 tablespoons water, approximately
250g boneless white fish fillets
250g scallops
¼ cup (60ml) mayonnaise
2 teaspoons grated lemon rind
300ml carton thickened cream
fresh dill sprigs, extra
thin strips lemon rind, extra

Sift flour into bowl, rub in butter, stir in dill, egg yolk and enough water to make ingredients cling together. Press dough into a ball, knead gently on lightly floured surface until smooth, cover; refrigerate 30 minutes.

Roll pastry between sheets of baking paper until 2mm thick. Cut pastry into rounds, using 6cm fluted cutter. Press rounds into 40 holes of shallow patty pans, lightly prick pastry with fork. Bake in moderate oven about 10 minutes or until lightly browned; cool.

Poach, steam or microwave fish and scallops until just cooked, drain; cool. Blend or process fish, scallops, mayonnaise and rind until smooth. Beat cream in small bowl until soft peaks form, fold into seafood mixture. Spoon seafood mixture into piping bag fitted with medium plain tube, pipe mixture into pastry cases; top with extra dill and extra rind.
Makes 40.

▨ Pastry cases and filling can be made 1 day ahead.
▨ Storage: Cases, in airtight container. Filling, covered, in refrigerator.
▨ Freeze: Not suitable.
▨ Microwave: Seafood suitable.

SMOKED FISH AND MUSTARD OMELETTE ROLLS

3 eggs, separated
¼ cup (20g) finely grated parmesan cheese
¼ cup (60ml) cream
1 teaspoon dry mustard
¼ teaspoon freshly ground black pepper

FILLING
350g smoked cod
¼ cup finely chopped fresh chives
⅓ cup (85g) mascarpone cheese
2 teaspoons lime juice
1 teaspoon dry mustard

Line base and sides of 26cm x 32cm Swiss roll pan with baking paper. Whisk egg yolks, cheese, cream, mustard and pepper in bowl until combined.

Beat egg whites in small bowl with electric mixer until soft peaks form; fold into yolk mixture in 2 batches. Spread

HERB SCONES WITH SMOKED TROUT

1¼ cups (185g) self-raising flour
30g butter, chopped
1 tablespoon chopped fresh sage
1 tablespoon chopped fresh chives
1 tablespoon chopped fresh dill
1 egg, lightly beaten
¾ cup (180ml) buttermilk, approximately
200g sliced smoked trout

FILLING
1 tablespoon horseradish cream
¼ cup (60ml) sour cream
1 tablespoon chopped fresh chives
150g camembert cheese

Sift flour into bowl, rub in butter, stir in herbs, egg and enough milk to mix to a sticky dough. Knead dough gently on floured surface until smooth, roll out until 1cm thick. Cut into 3.5cm rounds; place about 1cm apart on greased oven trays.

Bake in hot oven about 12 min until scones are browned; cool or Split scones in half, spoon filling bases, top with fish; replace tops.
Filling: Process all ingredients until combined, cover; refrigerate 1 hour. Makes about 40.

■ Filling can be made 2 days ahead.
■ Storage: Covered, in refrigerator.
■ Freeze: Scones suitable.
■ Microwave: Not suitable.

LEFT: From left: Smoked Fish and Mustard Omelette Rolls; Seafood Mousse in Pastry Cases.
BELOW: Herb Scones with Smoked Trout.

Left: China from Villeroy & Boch. Below: Glass plate from Villeroy & Boch; serviette ring from Morris Home & Garden Wares.

mixture into prepared pan. Bake in moderately hot oven about 8 minutes or until browned and puffed.

Turn omelette onto wire rack covered with tea-towel, carefully remove paper, cut omelette in half lengthways. Using tea-towels as a guide, roll up omelettes separately from long side. Unroll omelettes when cold, spread with filling, re-roll from long side. Wrap omelette rolls in plastic wrap; refrigerate until cold. Slice diagonally into 2cm pieces.
Filling: Poach, steam or microwave fish until tender, drain; cool. Remove skin and bones from fish. Transfer fish to bowl, flake with fork, stir in chives, cheese, juice and mustard.
Makes about 30.

■ Recipe can be made a day ahead.
■ Storage: Covered, in refrigerator.
■ Freeze: Not suitable.
■ Microwave: Fish suitable.

Palmiers

If you are planning ahead, palmiers can be prepared a day in advance. Place on prepared oven trays, cover tightly and refrigerate until required. Palmiers are best cooked as close to serving time as possible. Cooking times will vary a little depending on the type of filling chosen; check after 15 minutes, then continue to cook until browned as desired. Each recipe makes about 30 palmiers; none is suitable to freeze or microwave.

You need 2 sheets of ready-rolled puff pastry for each of the following 5 recipes. Spread half of each filling on 1 sheet of pastry; use the same method for each filling as shown below.

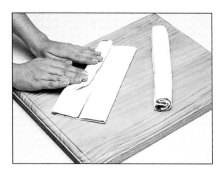

After filling mixture is spread on sheet of pastry, fold in sides to meet in centre, flatten slightly. Fold in half again, flatten slightly; press sides together. Cover, refrigerate 1 hour. Cut pastry into 1.5cm slices; place, cut side up, on lightly greased oven trays. Bake in moderately hot oven about 15 minutes.

KUMARA, SUN-DRIED TOMATO AND BASIL

You need to cook about 400g kumara for this recipe.

1 cup (320g) cold mashed kumara
1 clove garlic, crushed
2 teaspoons melted butter
½ cup sun-dried tomatoes in oil, drained, chopped
2 tablespoons chopped fresh basil

Combine all ingredients in bowl; mix well.

SPINACH AND FETA

3 bacon rashers, finely chopped
125g frozen chopped spinach, thawed
200g feta cheese, finely crumbled
¼ teaspoon ground nutmeg

Add bacon to pan, cook, stirring, until browned; drain. Squeeze moisture from spinach. Combine all ingredients in bowl; mix well.

PEANUT CORIANDER

⅓ cup (85g) crunchy peanut butter
⅓ cup (40g) ground almonds
¼ cup chopped fresh coriander leaves
1½ tablespoons mild curry paste

Combine all ingredients in bowl; mix well.

CHEESE, OLIVE AND ROSEMARY

100g packaged cream cheese, softened
2 teaspoons finely chopped fresh rosemary
¼ cup (60ml) olive paste

Combine cheese and rosemary in bowl; spread over half of each pastry sheet. Spread olive paste over other half of each pastry sheet.

MEXICAN-STYLE

1 large (350g) red pepper
⅓ cup (95g) canned refried beans
½ cup (35g) stale breadcrumbs
130g can corn kernels, drained
2 tablespoons grated tasty cheddar cheese
¼ cup chopped fresh coriander leaves

Quarter pepper, remove seeds and membranes. Grill pepper, skin side up, until skin blisters and blackens. Peel away skin, chop pepper finely. Combine all ingredients in bowl; mix well.

1. Peanut Coriander 2. Cheese, Olive and Rosemary 3. Mexican-Style 4. Kumara, Sun-Dried Tomato and Basil 5. Spinach and Feta.

China and glasses from House.

Preserved and Marinated Savouries

Preserved lemons are best made 3 weeks ahead and stored in a cool, dark place; turn jar every 3 days. Feta, sun-dried tomatoes and all olive recipes are best made 3 days ahead; store in refrigerator up to 2 weeks. Mushrooms are best made 3 hours ahead; store in refrigerator up to 2 days. All recipes are unsuitable to freeze or microwave.

MARINATED SWEET AND SOUR OLIVES

600g kalamata olives, drained
2 tablespoons finely chopped fresh lemon grass
3 lemon slices, halved
1¼ cups (310ml) olive oil
½ cup (125ml) mild sweet chilli sauce
¼ cup (60ml) white vinegar

Place olives, lemon grass and lemon slices into sterilised jar (1 litre/4 cup capacity). Gently heat oil, sauce and vinegar in pan until warm. Pour enough oil mixture into jar to cover olives completely; seal while hot.

MARINATED FRENCH OLIVES

600g large green olives, drained
1 cup (250ml) olive oil
½ cup (125ml) white wine vinegar
½ cup (125ml) fresh orange juice
2 teaspoons drained green peppercorns
3 bay leaves
2 fresh rosemary sprigs
2 teaspoons dried French gourmet herbs
2 cloves garlic, sliced

Place olives into sterilised jar (1 litre/ 4 cup capacity). Gently heat oil, vinegar and juice in pan until warm, add peppercorns, bay leaves, herbs and garlic. Pour enough oil mixture into jar to cover olives completely; seal while hot.

MARINATED CITRUS OLIVES

600g kalamata olives, drained
1½ cups (375ml) olive oil
¼ cup (60ml) fresh orange juice
¼ cup (60ml) fresh lemon juice
2 tablespoons chopped fresh dill
1 tablespoon black peppercorns
3 strips orange rind
3 strips lemon rind

Place olives into sterilised jar (1 litre/ 4 cup capacity). Gently heat oil and

juices in pan until warm, add dill, peppercorns and rinds. Pour enough oil mixture into jar to cover olives completely; seal while hot.

MARINATED HOT AND SPICY MEXICAN OLIVES

400g kalamata olives, drained
200g large green olives, drained
4 small fresh red chillies
1³/4 cups (430ml) olive oil
1/4 cup (60ml) red wine vinegar
3 small fresh red chillies, finely
   sliced, extra
3 sprigs fresh oregano
2 cloves garlic, halved
1 teaspoon cracked
   black pepper

Place olives and chillies into sterilised jar (1 litre/4 cup capacity). Gently heat oil and vinegar in pan until warm, add extra chillies, oregano, garlic and pepper. Pour enough oil mixture into jar to cover olives completely; seal while hot.

MARINATED MOROCCAN OLIVES

600g large green olives, drained
2 cups (500ml) olive oil
1 teaspoon cumin seeds
1 teaspoon coriander seeds
1/2 teaspoon fennel seeds
4 cardamom pods, bruised
2 cinnamon sticks
1/2 teaspoon ground nutmeg
3 strips lemon rind
2 cloves garlic, crushed

Place olives into sterilised jar (1 litre/4 cup capacity). Gently heat oil in pan until warm, add spices, rind and garlic. Pour enough oil mixture into jar to cover olives completely; seal while hot.

MARINATED SUN-DRIED TOMATOES

2 x 125g packets sun-dried
   tomato halves
1¹/2 cups (375ml) olive oil
1/2 cup (125ml) red wine vinegar
2 teaspoons cracked black pepper
2 teaspoons drained green
   peppercorns
2 teaspoons dried thyme leaves
10 fresh basil leaves
3 cloves garlic, sliced

Place tomatoes in large heatproof bowl, cover with hot water, stand 1 minute, drain; pat dry with absorbent paper. Pack tomatoes into sterilised jar (1 litre/4 cup capacity). Heat oil and vinegar in pan until hot; add peppers, herbs and garlic. Pour enough oil mixture into jar to cover tomatoes completely; seal while hot.

PRESERVED LEMONS

You will need about 30 large lemons for this recipe.

10 large (1.8kg) lemons
1/4 cup coarse cooking salt
2 cinnamon sticks
2 teaspoons cardamom seeds
1 teaspoon black peppercorns
1 teaspoon brown mustard seeds
5 cloves
2 bay leaves
1.5 litres (6 cups) fresh lemon juice,
   approximately

Quarter lemons lengthways, to within 5mm of the base. Open out lemons, sprinkle cut surfaces with salt; reshape lemons. Pack lemons firmly into sterilised jar (3 litre/12 cup capacity); add spices and bay leaves. Pour enough juice into jar to cover lemons completely; seal jar. To serve lemons, remove and discard pulp from rind, rinse rind; slice thinly.

MARINATED MUSHROOMS

350g button mushrooms
1¹/4 cups (310ml) olive oil
1/2 cup (125ml) fresh orange juice
1/2 cup (125ml) white
   wine vinegar
10 thin strips orange rind
2 teaspoons dried crushed chillies
1 teaspoon cracked black pepper
4 fresh sage leaves
5 small garlic cloves, halved

Wipe mushrooms with damp cloth. Place mushrooms into sterilised jar (1 litre/4 cup capacity). Heat oil, juice and vinegar in pan until hot, add rind, chillies, pepper, sage and garlic. Pour enough oil mixture into jar to cover mushrooms completely; seal while hot.

MARINATED FETA

650g feta cheese
1¹/4 cups (310ml) olive oil
1/4 cup (60ml) mild sweet
   chilli sauce
1/2 cup (125ml) white
   wine vinegar
2 teaspoons drained tiny capers
3 teaspoons cumin seeds
6 sprigs fresh thyme
2 teaspoons cracked black pepper
4 lime slices, halved

Cut cheese into 2cm cubes, gently rinse under cold water; drain. Place cheese into sterilised jar (1 litre/4 cup capacity). Heat oil, sauce and vinegar in pan until hot; add capers, seeds, thyme, pepper and lime. Pour enough oil mixture into jar to cover cheese completely; seal while hot.

1. Marinated Mushrooms 2. Marinated Sweet and Sour Olives 3. Marinated Hot and Spicy Mexican Olives 4. Marinated Moroccan Olives 5. Marinated Citrus Olives 6. Marinated French Olives 7. Marinated Feta 8. Marinated Sun-Dried Tomatoes 9. Preserved Lemons.

China and wire basket from Accoutrement; tiles from Country Floors.

PARMESAN PALMIERS WITH EGGPLANT DIP

½ cup (125g) soft cream cheese
½ cup (40g) finely grated
parmesan cheese
2 tablespoons chopped fresh chives
2 sheets ready-rolled puff pastry
2 tablespoons polenta

EGGPLANT DIP

1 large (500g) eggplant
6 cloves garlic
2 tablespoons plain yogurt
2 tablespoons sour cream
2 tablespoons chopped
fresh parsley
2 teaspoons lemon juice

Combine cheeses and chives in bowl; mix well. Spread cheese mixture over pastry sheets. Fold in sides of sheets to meet in centre, flatten gently, fold in half again, flatten gently, press together gently, cover; refrigerate 1 hour.

Cut pastry into 1cm slices, place, cut side up, on greased oven trays; sprinkle with polenta. Bake in moderately hot oven about 20 minutes or until browned; cool. Serve palmiers with eggplant dip.

Eggplant Dip: Place whole eggplant and unpeeled garlic on oven tray, bake, uncovered, in hot oven about 1 hour or until soft; cool 10 minutes. Peel eggplant and garlic, roughly chop eggplant flesh. Process eggplant and garlic with remaining ingredients until smooth, cover; refrigerate 3 hours or overnight. Makes about 40.

▓ Palmiers best made close to serving. Dip can be made 2 days ahead.
▓ Storage: Dip, covered, in refrigerator.
▓ Freeze: Not suitable.
▓ Microwave: Not suitable.

ABOVE: On platter: Parmesan Palmiers with Eggplant Dip; In jar: Cheesy Olive Twists. RIGHT: Chilli Cornbread Muffins.

Above: China from Corso De' Fiori.

CHEESY OLIVE TWISTS

4 sheets ready-rolled puff pastry
½ cup (125ml) sun-dried
tomato paste
2 cloves garlic, crushed
⅔ cup (80g) seeded black olives,
finely chopped
1 tablespoon chopped
fresh oregano
1 cup (125g) coarsely grated
tasty cheddar cheese
1 egg, lightly beaten

Spread pastry sheets with combined paste and garlic. Sprinkle half of each sheet with combined olives, oregano and cheese. Fold pastry sheets in half to cover olive mixture; press down firmly. Cut into 1.5cm strips crossways. Twist strips, place about 2cm apart on greased oven trays; brush with egg. Bake in hot oven about 12 minutes or until browned; cool on wire racks. Makes about 60.

CHILLI CORNBREAD MUFFINS

1 tablespoon olive oil
4 green shallots, finely chopped
1/4 cup chopped fresh
    coriander leaves
1/2 small (75g) red pepper,
    finely chopped
1 clove garlic, crushed
2 small fresh red chillies,
    finely chopped
1/2 teaspoon ground cumin
1 cup (170g) polenta
1/2 cup (75g) self-raising flour
1/2 teaspoon bicarbonate of soda
1 egg
1/2 cup (125ml) buttermilk
60g butter, melted

CORIANDER CREAM

3/4 cup (180ml) low-fat sour cream
1/2 teaspoon sambal oelek
1 tablespoon chopped fresh
    coriander leaves
1 green shallot, finely chopped

Heat oil in pan, add shallots, coriander, pepper, garlic, chillies and cumin, cook, stirring, until pepper is soft; transfer to bowl. Stir in polenta, sifted flour and soda, then combined remaining ingredients. Spoon mixture into greased 3 x 12 hole mini muffin pans (1 tablespoon capacity). Bake in moderately hot oven about 10 minutes or until browned. Turn muffins onto wire racks to cool, serve with coriander cream.

Coriander Cream: Combine all ingredients in bowl.
Makes about 36.

■ Muffins best made just before
    serving. Coriander cream can be
    made a day ahead.
■ Storage: Covered, in refrigerator.
■ Freeze: Muffins suitable.
■ Microwave: Not suitable.

■ Twists can be made a day ahead.
■ Storage: Airtight container.
■ Freeze: Uncooked unglazed
    twists suitable.
■ Microwave: Not suitable.

Bruschetta with Toppings

Each of the following toppings is enough for 1 bread stick. None is suitable to freeze or microwave. With the exception of the garlic and olive oil topping, the toppings can be prepared a day ahead and kept, covered, in the refrigerator; however, fresh herbs should be freshly chopped and added to each topping mixture just before serving. All topping ingredients need to be finely sliced or chopped to ensure they do not fall off bruschetta slices.

BRUSCHETTA

28cm long bread stick

Trim ends from bread stick, cut into 1cm slices, grill or toast until lightly browned. All toppings are enough for 1 bread stick, giving about 26 serves.

ZUCCHINI AND PINE NUT

2 tablespoons olive oil
1 tablespoon pine nuts
1 clove garlic, crushed
1 (60g) finger eggplant, chopped
1 medium (130g) tomato, chopped
2 small (180g) zucchini, chopped
6 seedless black olives, chopped
2 tablespoons sultanas
2 teaspoons red wine vinegar
1 tablespoon chopped fresh basil

Heat oil in pan, add nuts, garlic and eggplant, cook, stirring, 5 minutes. Add tomato, zucchini, olives, sultanas and vinegar, cook, stirring, until zucchini is soft; cool. Spoon vegetable mixture onto toasts; top with basil.

ROASTED RED PEPPER AND OLIVE

2 large (700g) red peppers
1 tablespoon lemon juice
2 teaspoons drained capers
1 clove garlic, crushed
1/4 cup chopped fresh parsley
1 teaspoon ground cumin
2 teaspoons sugar
1/3 cup (50g) seedless black olives, chopped
parmesan cheese shavings
fresh parsley sprigs, extra

Quarter peppers, remove seeds and membranes. Grill peppers, skin side up, until skin blisters and blackens. Peel away skin, blend or process roasted peppers with juice, capers, garlic, parsley, cumin and sugar until smooth. Stir in olives. Spoon pepper mixture onto toasts; top with cheese and extra parsley.

MINTED BEETROOT

1 large (200g) fresh beetroot
1½ tablespoons tahini
2 teaspoons lemon juice
1/4 cup (60ml) low-fat sour cream
1/4 cup (60ml) plain yogurt
1 clove garlic, crushed
1/4 cup chopped fresh mint
fresh mint leaves, extra

Boil, steam or microwave unpeeled beetroot until tender, drain; cool. Peel beetroot, chop roughly, blend or process with tahini, juice, cream, yogurt and garlic until smooth. Stir in 2 tablespoons of mint. Spoon beetroot mixture onto toasts; top with remaining mint and extra mint.

ROAST LAMB, EGGPLANT AND YOGURT

250g lamb fillets
2 tablespoons lemon pepper
2 tablespoons olive oil
3/4 cup (180ml) plain yogurt
1 tablespoon lemon juice
1 teaspoon sugar
1 clove garlic, crushed
2 tablespoons chopped fresh mint
13 slices bottled roasted eggplant, drained
fresh mint leaves, extra

Toss lamb in lemon pepper. Heat oil in pan, add lamb, cook until browned all over and tender; cool. Combine yogurt, juice, sugar, garlic and mint in bowl. Halve eggplant slices, place on toasts; top with thinly sliced lamb, yogurt mixture, then extra mint.

GOATS' CHEESE AND SUN-DRIED TOMATO

150g goats' cheese
1/4 cup (60ml) low-fat sour cream
2 teaspoons drained capers
1/2 teaspoon chopped fresh thyme
1/4 cup sun-dried tomatoes in oil, drained, chopped
fresh thyme leaves, extra

Blend or process cheese, cream, capers and thyme until just combined. Spoon cheese mixture onto toasts; top with tomatoes and extra thyme.

GARLIC AND OLIVE OIL

13 cloves garlic, halved
1 cup (250ml) olive oil, approximately
1 tablespoon chopped fresh parsley

Rub half a clove of garlic over 1 side of each piece of toast; lightly drizzle with oil, sprinkle with parsley.

ROAST BEEF AND HUMMUS

3/4 cup (180ml) hummus
1/4 cup (60ml) plain yogurt
1 teaspoon ground cumin
2 teaspoons lemon juice
1 small (150g) red pepper
200g rare roast beef, sliced
fresh oregano leaves

Combine hummus, yogurt, cumin and juice in bowl, cover; refrigerate 3 hours or overnight. Quarter pepper, remove seeds and membranes. Grill pepper, skin side up, until skin blisters and blackens. Peel away skin. Cut pepper into thin strips. Spoon hummus mixture onto toasts; top with beef, pepper and oregano leaves.

TOMATO AND BASIL

3 small (300g) tomatoes, chopped
1 small (100g) red Spanish onion,
    chopped
1/4 cup shredded fresh basil
2 tablespoons olive oil

Combine all ingredients in bowl; spoon onto toasts.

MIXED MUSHROOM

2 tablespoons olive oil
350g button mushrooms, sliced
250g Swiss brown mushrooms,
    sliced
3 cloves garlic, crushed
1 tablespoon lemon juice
1 tablespoon balsamic vinegar
1/4 cup chopped fresh chives
1/2 cup (40g) finely grated
    parmesan cheese

Heat oil in pan, add mushrooms and garlic, cook, stirring, 5 minutes. Add juice, vinegar and chives, cook, stirring, until liquid has evaporated; cool. Spoon mushroom mixture onto toasts; sprinkle with cheese.

1. *Spicy Eggplant* 2. *Mixed Mushroom*
3. *Minted Beetroot* 4. *Roast Beef and*
Hummus 5. *Roasted Red Pepper and Olive*
6. *Goats' Cheese and Sun-Dried Tomato*
7. *Roast Lamb, Eggplant and Yogurt*
8. *Zucchini and Pine Nut* 9. *Tomato and*
Basil 10. *Garlic and Olive Oil.*

Tiles from Country Floors.

SPICY EGGPLANT

2 tablespoons olive oil
1 small (80g) onion, chopped
1 clove garlic, crushed
1 teaspoon mild curry paste
1 teaspoon ground cumin
1 medium (130g) tomato, chopped
1 medium (300g) eggplant,
    peeled, chopped
1/2 cup (125ml) plain yogurt
1/4 cup chopped fresh
    coriander leaves

Heat half the oil in pan, add onion, garlic, paste and cumin, cook, stirring, until onion is soft. Add tomato, cook, stirring, 5 minutes; remove from pan. Add remaining oil to same pan, add eggplant, cook, stirring, until lightly browned. Stir in tomato mixture; cool. Combine yogurt in bowl with half the coriander. Spoon eggplant mixture onto toasts, top with yogurt mixture; sprinkle with remaining coriander.

ROE AND LEEK TOASTS

20g butter
1 clove garlic, crushed
1 small (200g) leek, thinly sliced
30cm bread stick
250g tub soft cream cheese
1 tablespoon chopped fresh thyme
1/4 teaspoon ground black pepper
1 tablespoon mayonnaise
1 teaspoon grated lemon rind
100g salmon roe

Melt butter in pan, add garlic and leek, cook, covered, over low heat until leek is soft; cool. Trim ends from bread, cut into 1cm slices, place in single layer on oven trays. Toast in moderate oven about 10 minutes or until browned on both sides; cool. Blend or process cheese, thyme, pepper, mayonnaise and rind until smooth. Spread cheese mixture over toasts; top with leek mixture and roe. Makes about 25.

■ Toasts and cheese mixture can be made 3 days ahead.
■ Storage: Toasts, in airtight container. Cheese mixture, covered, in refrigerator.
■ Freeze: Not suitable.
■ Microwave: Leek mixture suitable.

ABOVE: Roe and Leek Toasts.
RIGHT: From back: Herb and Blue Cheese Cigars; Steak Tartare Canapes.

Above: China and serviette from Villeroy & Boch; spoon, bowl and gold and silver beads from Morris Home & Garden Wares. Right: China from Villeroy & Boch; tea-towel and glasses from Morris Home & Garden Wares.

HERB AND BLUE CHEESE CIGARS

You will need to cook about 2/3 cup (130g) short-grain rice for this recipe.

2 teaspoons soft butter
2 medium (300g) onions, finely chopped
300g blue vein cheese, crumbled
1/2 cup (40g) finely grated parmesan cheese
1 tablespoon chopped fresh parsley
2 tablespoons chopped fresh basil
1 tablespoon chopped fresh coriander leaves
2 cups cooked short-grain rice
20 sheets fillo pastry
125g butter, melted, extra

Melt butter in pan, add onions, cook, covered, over low heat until onions are soft; cool. Combine onion mixture, cheeses, herbs and rice in bowl; mix well.

Cut a sheet of fillo in half lengthways, fold in half lengthways; brush with some of the extra butter. Place a tablespoon of cheese mixture at 1 end of pastry, roll up, brush with a little more butter, place on oven tray. Repeat with remaining pastry, cheese mixture and butter. Bake in moderately hot oven about 15 minutes or until lightly browned. Serve hot or cold. Makes 40.

■ Recipe can be made 3 hours ahead.
■ Storage: Covered, in refrigerator.
■ Freeze: Uncooked rolls suitable.
■ Microwave: Rice and onion mixture suitable.

STEAK TARTARE CANAPES

14 slices wholegrain bread
1/2 cup (125ml) mayonnaise
1 tablespoon Dijon mustard
300g beef eye-fillet steak, chopped
1 tablespoon drained capers, chopped
2 gherkins, finely chopped
2 teaspoons Worcestershire sauce
1/2 small (40g) onion, finely chopped
1 tablespoon olive oil
2 teaspoons Dijon mustard, extra
1 tablespoon chopped fresh parsley
fresh parsley sprigs, extra
freshly ground black pepper

Cut 4 x 4cm rounds from each slice of bread; toast or grill until browned on both sides. Combine mayonnaise and mustard in bowl; mix well.

Process steak until finely minced, combine in bowl with capers, gherkins, sauce, onion, oil, extra mustard and parsley; mix well. Shape teaspoons of mixture into patties. Spread toasts with mustard mayonnaise; top with patties. Top with extra parsley and pepper. Makes 56.

■ Steak mixture best made just before serving. Toasts and mayonnaise mixture can be made 2 days ahead.
■ Storage: Toasts, in airtight container. Mayonnaise mixture, covered, in refrigerator.
■ Freeze: Not suitable.
■ Microwave: Not suitable.

Nutty Savoury Nibbles

Each of these 10 recipes can be stored in an airtight container but none is suitable to freeze or microwave. The Cajun bacon popcorn can be made 3 hours ahead of serving; the rosemary pretzels can be made 1 day ahead; and the rest can be made up to a month ahead.

MIDDLE EASTERN MIX

2 cups (300g) unroasted hazelnuts
1 egg white
1 tablespoon cumin seeds
2 teaspoons ground cinnamon
½ cup (80g) pine nuts
½ cup (75g) dried apricots,
  finely sliced
1 teaspoon ground coriander
1 teaspoon salt

Place hazelnuts on oven tray, bake in moderate oven 15 minutes; cool. Rub off skins, using tea-towel. Whisk egg white in large bowl until frothy, stir in all ingredients. Spread mixture onto greased oven tray. Bake in moderate oven, stirring occasionally, about 25 minutes or until mixture is dry and crisp.
Makes about 3 cups.

CURRIED SESAME ALMONDS

1 tablespoon sesame oil
2 cups (320g) blanched almonds
¼ cup (35g) sesame seeds
1½ tablespoons mild curry powder
2 teaspoons salt
¼ teaspoon ground turmeric
⅓ cup (55g) sultanas

Heat oil in pan, add nuts, cook, stirring, until lightly browned. Add seeds, curry powder, salt and turmeric, cook, stirring, until seeds are lightly browned; cool. Stir in sultanas.
Makes about 2½ cups.

ORANGE SPICED NUTS

1 medium (180g) orange
1 egg white
½ teaspoon ground cardamom
¼ cup (55g) caster sugar
3 cups (300g) pecans
½ cup (75g) pistachios
1 cup (50g) flaked coconut, toasted

Using a vegetable peeler, carefully remove rind from orange; cut rind into thin strips. Whisk egg white in large bowl until frothy, stir in rind, cardamom, sugar and nuts. Spread mixture onto greased oven tray, bake in moderate oven, stirring occasionally, about 30 minutes or until crisp and browned; cool. Stir in coconut.
Makes about 4½ cups.

DEVILLED NUTS

1 egg white
1 cup (160g) blanched almonds,
  toasted
½ cup (75g) unsalted
  roasted cashews
1½ cups (225g) unsalted
  roasted peanuts
1½ cups (150g) pecans
1½ teaspoons garlic powder
1 tablespoon Worcestershire sauce
2 teaspoons chilli powder
1 tablespoon sweet paprika
1½ teaspoons salt
1 teaspoon mild curry powder

Whisk egg white in large bowl until frothy, stir in remaining ingredients. Spread mixture onto greased oven tray. Bake in moderate oven, stirring occasionally, about 20 minutes or until mixture is dry and crisp; cool.
Makes about 4½ cups.

PEPITA AND KUMARA MIX

1 small (250g) kumara, peeled
2 cups (320g) pepitas
½ cup (80g) sunflower seed kernels
1 teaspoon cracked black pepper
3 teaspoons sea salt flakes
2 teaspoons salt-reduced soy sauce

Using a vegetable peeler, peel thin strips from kumara, place in single layer over baking paper-covered oven trays. Bake in slow oven, turning occasionally, about 1 hour or until kumara is crisp. Combine remaining ingredients in large bowl; spread onto lightly greased oven tray. Bake in moderate oven about 20 minutes or until mixture is lightly browned; cool. Combine seed mixture with kumara in bowl; mix well
Makes about 3½ cups.

GINGER MACADAMIA MIX

30g piece fresh ginger, peeled
2 cups (300g) macadamias
1 cup (140g) slivered almonds
¾ teaspoon five spice powder
⅓ cup (50g) pistachios
1 teaspoon vegetable oil

Peel thin strips from ginger using a vegetable peeler. Combine ginger with remaining ingredients in bowl; mix

well. Spread mixture onto greased oven tray. Bake in moderate oven, stirring occasionally, about 20 minutes or until browned; cool.
Makes about 3 cups.

FRIED DELIGHTS

60g coloured prawn crackers
4 (30g) tikka pappadums
4 (40g) tandoori pappadums
vegetable oil for deep-frying
½ cup (85g) brazil nuts
1 cup (150g) roasted chickpeas
½ teaspoon five spice powder
½ teaspoon crushed dried chillies

Break crackers and both types of pappadums separately into small pieces. Deep-fry crackers and pappadums separately in batches in hot oil until puffed; drain on absorbent paper. Deep-fry nuts and chickpeas separately in batches in hot oil until lightly browned; drain on absorbent paper. Rub off skins of nuts, using tea-towel. Combine crackers, pappadums, nuts and chickpeas with remaining ingredients in large bowl; mix gently.
Makes about 11 cups.

ROSEMARY PRETZEL MIX

⅔ loaf (about 400g) unsliced
  white bread
1 teaspoon chicken salt
2 tablespoons chopped
  fresh rosemary
2 teaspoons sweet paprika
¼ cup (30g) finely grated
  gruyere cheese
100g butter, melted
2 cups (45g) puffed corn, toasted
125g packet stick pretzels, halved
1 cup (150g) unsalted
  roasted peanuts

Remove crust from bread, cut bread into 1.5cm cubes. Combine bread, salt, rosemary, paprika, cheese and butter in large bowl; mix well. Spread bread mixture over greased oven trays. Bake in moderate oven, stirring occasionally, about 50 minutes or until browned and crisp; cool. Combine bread mixture with remaining ingredients in large bowl.
Makes about 10 cups.

ASIAN-STYLE MIX

1½ cups (225g) unsalted
 raw cashews
1½ cups (150g) walnuts
2 teaspoons grated fresh ginger
1½ tablespoons mild sweet
 chilli sauce
2 cloves garlic, crushed
1 tablespoon salt-reduced soy sauce

Place cashews on oven tray, bake in moderate oven about 15 minutes or until lightly browned; cool. Combine cashews with remaining ingredients in large bowl. Spread nut mixture onto greased oven tray. Bake in moderate oven, stirring occasionally, about 20 minutes or until crisp; cool.
Makes about 3 cups.

CAJUN BACON POPCORN

8 bacon rashers, chopped
2 tablespoons olive oil
¾ cup (170g) popping corn
2 cups (160g) coarsely grated
 parmesan cheese
¼ cup dried parsley flakes
1½ tablespoons Cajun seasoning

Add bacon to non-stick pan, cook, stirring, until browned and crisp; drain on absorbent paper. Heat oil in large deep pan, add corn, cook, covered with tight-fitting lid, over low heat until corn has popped. Transfer popcorn to large bowl; stand 10 minutes. Stir in bacon, cheese, parsley and seasoning.
Makes about 11 cups.

1. Middle Eastern Mix 2. Curried Sesame Almonds 3. Pepita and Kumara Mix 4. Ginger Macadamia Mix 5. Devilled Nuts 6. Cajun Bacon Popcorn 7. Rosemary Pretzel Mix 8. Asian-Style Mix 9. Fried Delights 10. Orange Spiced Nuts.

Glasses from Home & Garden on the Mall; serving dishes from House.

ROSTI WITH SOUR CREAM AND CHIVES

30g butter
4 green shallots, chopped
1 clove garlic, crushed
1 small (250g) kumara, grated
1 medium (200g) potato, grated
1/3 cup (50g) pine nuts,
 toasted, chopped
1 egg, lightly beaten
1/4 cup (35g) plain flour
2 tablespoons vegetable oil
toasted pine nuts, extra
chopped fresh chives

CHIVE CREAM
1/2 cup (125ml) sour cream
2 tablespoons finely chopped
 fresh chives
1 teaspoon freshly ground
 black pepper

Heat butter in pan, add shallots, garlic, kumara, potato and pine nuts, cook, stirring, until potato is sticky; cool. Stir in egg and flour. Shape rounded teaspoons of mixture into balls, using floured fingers; flatten slightly. Heat oil in pan, add rosti, cook about 1 minute each side or until browned; drain. Serve topped with chive cream, extra pine nuts and chives.
Chive Cream: Combine all ingredients in bowl; mix well.
Makes about 35.

▨ Recipe best made just
 before serving.
▨ Freeze: Not suitable.
▨ Microwave: Not suitable.

SMOKED TROUT PINWHEELS

1 cup (150g) plain flour
4 eggs, lightly beaten
1 tablespoon vegetable oil
1 cup (250ml) milk
1½ tablespoons chopped
 fresh parsley
1 tablespoon grated lemon rind

FILLING
300g smoked trout, flaked
1 tablespoon chopped fresh dill
1 teaspoon chopped fresh
 lemon thyme
2/3 cup (170g) mascarpone cheese

Sift flour into bowl, gradually stir in combined eggs, oil, milk, parsley and rind, beat until smooth. Cover; stand 30 minutes. Pour 2 to 3 tablespoons batter into heated greased heavy-based crepe pan,

cook until lightly browned underneath. Turn crepe, brown on other side. Repeat with remaining batter. You will need 10 crepes for this recipe. Place 2 crepes, slightly overlapping, on board. Spread a fifth of filling onto crepes, covering surface; roll up firmly from short side. Repeat with remaining crepes and filling. Wrap rolls, individually, in plastic wrap; refrigerate 1 hour. Remove plastic wrap, trim ends from rolls, cut into 1cm slices.
Filling: Combine all ingredients in bowl; mix well.
Makes about 50.

■ Crepe rolls can be prepared a day ahead.
■ Storage: Covered, in refrigerator.
■ Freeze: Crepes suitable.
■ Microwave: Not suitable.

FRESH SPRING ROLLS

2 teaspoons peanut oil
2 teaspoons grated fresh ginger
2 cloves garlic, crushed
5 green shallots, chopped
250g minced pork
350g uncooked medium prawns, shelled, chopped
2 tablespoons chopped fresh mint
1 tablespoon fish sauce
2 tablespoons mild sweet chilli sauce
1 tablespoon lime juice
½ teaspoon sugar
30 x 16cm round rice paper sheets

CHILLI SAUCE
1 cup (220g) sugar
½ cup (125ml) water
½ cup (125ml) lime juice
2 tablespoons mild sweet chilli sauce
1 tablespoon chopped fresh coriander leaves
2 small fresh red chillies, chopped

Heat oil in pan, add ginger, garlic and shallots, cook, stirring, until shallots are soft. Add pork and prawns, cook, stirring, until prawns have changed colour and pork is tender. Stir in mint, sauces, juice and sugar, cook, stirring, a few minutes or until liquid has evaporated; cool. Place rice sheets, 1 at a time, in large bowl of water, soak 3 minutes or until sheets have softened; gently lift from water, place on board. Cut sheets in half, place 1 teaspoon pork mixture on corner of each half, fold in sides, roll up to enclose filling. Repeat with remaining pork mixture and rice paper. Serve with chilli sauce.
Chilli Sauce: Place sugar and water in small pan, stir over heat, without boiling, until sugar is dissolved; simmer, uncovered, without stirring, about 5 minutes or until mixture thickens slightly. Stir in remaining ingredients; cool.
Makes 60.

■ Rolls can be made 1 hour ahead. Sauce can be made a day ahead.
■ Storage: Rolls, covered with damp cloth and plastic wrap, in refrigerator. Sauce, covered, in refrigerator.
■ Freeze: Not suitable.
■ Microwave: Not suitable.

LEFT: From top: Smoked Trout Pinwheels; Rosti with Sour Cream and Chives.
ABOVE: Fresh Spring Rolls.

Left: China from Villeroy & Boch; coasters from Morris Home & Garden Wares.

A Selection of Pikelets

The addition of different foods to flavour a basic pikelet mixture, plus a topping to complement each variation, makes an interesting canape platter. Each of the following topping recipes is enough for 50 pikelets (1 quantity of basic pikelet mixture); prepare each as directed. Cooked pikelets can be made 2 days ahead and stored, covered, in refrigerator; they are also suitable to freeze, but not suitable to microwave. Pikelets are best assembled with toppings just before serving. None of the toppings is suitable to freeze or microwave.

BASIC PIKELET MIXTURE

¾ cup (110g) self-raising flour
1 teaspoon sugar
1 egg, lightly beaten
⅔ cup (180ml) milk
20g butter, melted

Sift flour and sugar into bowl, gradually stir in combined egg and milk, mix to a smooth batter. Stir in butter. Drop teaspoons of mixture into heated greased heavy-based pan, cook until bubbles appear; turn pikelets, brown other side. Makes about 50.

DILL PIKELETS WITH SMOKED SALMON SCRAMBLED EGGS

1 tablespoon chopped fresh dill
2 teaspoons drained capers,
    finely chopped
6 eggs, lightly beaten
½ cup (125ml) cream
70g sliced smoked salmon,
    finely chopped
2 tablespoons chopped fresh chives
10g soft butter
dill sprigs, extra

Stir dill and capers into basic pikelet mixture; make pikelets. Whisk eggs, cream, salmon and chives together in bowl. Melt butter in pan, add egg mixture, cook over low heat, stirring gently, until eggs are creamy and just set. Spoon onto pikelets; top with extra dill.

SAFFRON CORN PIKELETS WITH REFRIED BEANS

2 x 130g cans corn kernels, drained
pinch saffron powder
½ cup (125g) canned refried beans
⅔ cup (160ml) bottled mild salsa
2 green shallots, finely chopped
1 tablespoon finely chopped fresh
    coriander leaves
⅔ cup (80g) grated tasty
    cheddar cheese
red pepper strips

Stir corn and saffron into basic pikelet mixture; make pikelets and spread with refried beans. Combine salsa, shallots and coriander in bowl; spoon onto pikelets, sprinkle with cheese. Grill until cheese melts; top with red pepper strips.

WHOLEMEAL PIKELETS WITH ROASTED VEGETABLES

½ cup (75g) white self-raising flour
¼ cup (40g) wholemeal
    self-raising flour
1 (60g) finger eggplant, sliced
1 tablespoon olive oil
1 medium (200g) red pepper
20g butter
1 small (200g) leek, chopped
2 teaspoons chopped fresh basil
⅓ cup (80ml) olive paste

Substitute white and wholemeal self-raising flours for flour in basic pikelet mixture and stir in about 1 tablespoon extra milk; make pikelets. Place eggplant slices on oven tray, brush with oil. Bake in moderate oven about 15 minutes or until tender; cool. Slice into strips. Quarter pepper, remove seeds and membranes. Grill pepper, skin side up, until skin blisters and blackens. Peel away skin, slice pepper thinly. Heat butter in pan, add leek and basil, cook, stirring, until leek is soft; stir in eggplant and pepper. Spread pikelets with olive paste; top with roasted vegetables.

BASIC PIKELETS WITH QUAIL EGGS AND ANCHOVIES

⅔ cup (160ml) mayonnaise
1 teaspoon lemon juice
1 tablespoon finely chopped
    fresh chives
13 hard-boiled quail eggs, quartered
2 x 45g cans anchovy fillets, drained,
    finely sliced
1 green shallot

Make basic pikelets and spread with combined mayonnaise, juice and chives; top with eggs, anchovies and fine strips of shallot.

OLIVE PIKELETS WITH CRISPY PROSCIUTTO

⅓ cup (25g) grated
    parmesan cheese
½ cup (60g) seedless black olives,
    finely chopped
13 slices (195g) prosciutto
⅔ cup (170g) mascarpone cheese
¼ cup chopped fresh oregano

Stir parmesan and olives into basic pikelet mixture; make pikelets. Cut prosciutto into quarters, thread onto metal skewers, grill until browned and crisp. Remove prosciutto while warm. Spread pikelets with combined mascarpone and oregano; top with prosciutto.

BEETROOT PIKELETS WITH CITRUS CHIVE CHEESE

1 baby (20g) beetroot
½ teaspoon ground nutmeg
2 x 250g packets cream cheese,
    softened
2 tablespoons chopped fresh chives
1 tablespoon grated orange rind
2 tablespoons orange juice
fresh chives, extra
orange rind, extra

Boil, steam or microwave beetroot until just tender; peel, cool. Grate beetroot finely, drain on absorbent paper, then stir into basic pikelet mixture with nutmeg; make pikelets. Beat cheese in bowl, beat in chives, rind and juice. Spoon topping onto pikelets; top with extra snipped chives and thin strips of extra orange rind.

1. Basic Pikelets with Quail Eggs and Anchovies 2. Saffron Corn Pikelets with Refried Beans 3. Beetroot Pikelets with Citrus Chive Cheese 4. Dill Pikelets with Smoked Salmon Scrambled Eggs 5. Olive Pikelets with Crispy Prosciutto 6. Wholemeal Pikelets with Roasted Vegetables 7. Dill Pikelets with Smoked Salmon Scrambled Eggs.

Platters from House; glasses and serviettes from Home & Garden on the Mall.

POLENTA ROUNDS WITH SOUR CREAM AND SALAMI

3 cups (750ml) vegetable stock
1 cup (170g) polenta
½ cup (40g) finely grated
**   parmesan cheese**
¼ cup finely chopped fresh basil
¼ cup (40g) polenta, extra
2 tablespoons olive oil
100g sliced salami, thinly sliced
300ml sour cream
½ cup (125ml) thickened cream
2 small fresh red chillies,
**   finely chopped**
½ teaspoon cracked black pepper
fresh dill sprigs

Grease 26cm x 32cm Swiss roll pan, line base and sides with baking paper. Bring stock to boil in medium pan, gradually add polenta, simmer, stirring, about 10 minutes or until soft and thick. Stir in cheese and basil. Spread mixture into prepared pan; cool. Cover polenta; refrigerate until firm.

Cut 3.5cm rounds from polenta, coat rounds in extra polenta. Heat oil in pan, cook rounds in batches until lightly browned on both sides, drain; cool. Grill salami until crisp, drain; cool. Combine sour cream, cream, chillies and pepper in small bowl. Top polenta rounds with cream mixture, salami strips and dill. Makes about 60.

■ Recipe can be made 3 hours ahead.
■ Storage: Covered, in refrigerator.
■ Freeze: Not suitable.
■ Microwave: Not suitable.

CRAB PATTIES WITH CHILLI PIMIENTO SAUCE

170g can crab meat, drained
¼ cup (60ml) mayonnaise
1 teaspoon grated lime rind
1 tablespoon chopped fresh coriander leaves
2 green shallots, finely chopped
1 cup (70g) stale breadcrumbs
1 egg, lightly beaten
plain flour
vegetable oil for shallow-frying

CHILLI PIMIENTO SAUCE
¼ cup finely chopped canned drained pimientos
¼ cup (60ml) mayonnaise
1 teaspoon sambal oelek

Place crab meat on absorbent paper, squeeze out excess moisture. Combine crab meat, mayonnaise, rind, coriander, shallots, breadcrumbs and egg in bowl. Shape rounded teaspoons of mixture into balls, flatten slightly; toss in flour. Shallow-fry patties in batches in hot oil until lightly browned; drain. Serve patties with chilli pimiento sauce.

Chilli Pimiento Sauce: Drain pimientos on absorbent paper. Process pimientos with remaining ingredients until smooth. Makes about 30.

▓ Crab patties and sauce can be made a day ahead.
▓ Storage: Covered, separately, in refrigerator.
▓ Freeze: Cooked patties suitable.
▓ Microwave: Not suitable.

ABOVE: Crab Patties with Chilli Pimiento Sauce.
RIGHT: Polenta Rounds with Sour Cream and Salami.

Right: China from Villeroy & Boch.

Dips and Dippers

These dips can be made 3 days ahead and stored, covered, in refrigerator. None is suitable to freeze or microwave. The puff pastry cheese straws, cheesy pita crisps and focaccia sticks can be made a day ahead and stored in airtight containers. Before cooking, these are suitable to freeze; none is suitable to microwave. Any suitable vegetables can be cut into sticks for a fresh, crunchy platter. Packet grissini (bread sticks) also make great dippers.

CHILLI RED PEPPER

2 small (300g) red peppers
1/4 cup (60ml) lime juice
1 cup (70g) stale breadcrumbs
2 small fresh red chillies, chopped
4 cloves garlic, chopped
1 small (100g) red Spanish onion, chopped

Quarter peppers, remove seeds and membranes. Grill peppers, skin side up, until skin blisters and blackens. Peel away skin. Blend or process peppers with remaining ingredients.
Makes about 1 3/4 cups (430ml).

CHICKPEA

2 x 300g cans chickpeas, rinsed, drained
2 tablespoons tahini
1/4 cup fresh mint leaves
1 teaspoon ground cumin
1/3 cup (80ml) lemon juice
2 cloves garlic, chopped
1/2 teaspoon hot paprika
few drops Tabasco sauce
1/4 cup (60ml) plain yogurt

Blend or process all ingredients until mixture is smooth.
Makes about 2 1/2 cups (625ml).

CURRIED MANGO

1 teaspoon peanut oil
1 small (80g) onion, chopped
2 cloves garlic, crushed
2 teaspoons mild curry powder
1 medium (430g) mango, chopped
2 tablespoons mayonnaise
1 tablespoon French onion soup mix
250g packet cream cheese, chopped

Heat oil in pan, add onion, garlic and curry powder; cook, stirring, until onion is soft. Blend or process mixture with remaining ingredients until smooth.
Makes about 2 1/2 cups (625ml).

CAVIAR

6 slices white bread
375g packaged cream cheese, chopped
100g lumpfish roe caviar
1 tablespoon lemon juice

Remove crusts from bread. Place bread in bowl, cover with cold water, stand 5 minutes; drain, press water from bread. Blend or process bread with remaining ingredients until smooth.
Makes about 2 cups (500ml).

MUSTARD CREAM

3 egg yolks
2 tablespoons lemon juice
125g butter, melted
1 teaspoon French mustard
1 tablespoon chopped fresh parsley
250g tub light cream cheese, chopped

Blend or process egg yolks and juice until just combined. Add butter gradually in a thin stream while motor is operating. Add mustard, parsley and cheese, blend or process until smooth.
Makes about 2 cups (500ml).

FOCACCIA STICKS

16cm x 22cm piece focaccia
3/4 cup (180ml) olive oil
1 teaspoon cracked black pepper
1 teaspoon garlic salt
1 tablespoon dried basil leaves

Split focaccia in half, cut each half into 3 pieces; cut each piece into 10 sticks. Brush top and sides of each stick with oil; sprinkle with combined pepper, salt and basil, place on oven trays. Bake in moderately hot oven about 15 minutes or until browned and crisp.
Makes 60.

CHEESY PITA CRISPS

5 large pita pocket breads
1/4 cup (60ml) olive oil
2/3 cup (50g) finely grated parmesan cheese
1 teaspoon cracked black pepper

Split each pita bread in half, cut each half into quarters. Place bread in single layer on oven trays; brush with oil. Sprinkle with combined cheese and pepper. Bake in moderately hot oven about 10 minutes or until browned and crisp.
Makes 40.

PUFF PASTRY CHEESE STRAWS

2 sheets ready-rolled puff pastry
1 egg, lightly beaten
1/2 cup (40g) finely grated parmesan cheese

Brush pastry sheets with egg; sprinkle 1 sheet with cheese. Top with other pastry sheet; press together. Cut into 1.5cm strips, cut each strip in half.

Twist strips, place about 2cm apart on greased oven trays. Bake in moderately hot oven about 12 minutes or until strips are lightly browned.
Makes about 30.

1. Caviar *2.* Mustard Cream *3.* Chickpea
4. Curried Mango *5.* Cheesy Pita Crisps
6. Puff Pastry Cheese Straws *7.* Focaccia
Sticks *8.* Chilli Red Pepper.

Setting from Corso De' Fiori.

33

CHICKEN AND PROSCIUTTO ROULADE TOASTS

8 slices white bread
3 (500g) chicken breast fillets
¼ cup (60ml) sun-dried tomato paste
6 slices (90g) prosciutto
1 tablespoon olive oil
⅓ cup (80ml) mayonnaise
fresh thyme leaves

Remove crusts from bread, cut into 4 x 4.5cm squares from each slice of bread, place on oven tray. Toast in moderate oven about 15 minutes or until browned and crisp; cool. Place chicken between sheets of plastic wrap, then place, smooth side down, on board, pound gently with meat mallet to flatten slightly. Spread paste over chicken, top chicken with prosciutto, roll up from the short side, secure with toothpicks. Heat oil in pan, add chicken, cook, covered, over low heat, turning occasionally, until browned and cooked through, drain on absorbent paper; cool. Discard toothpicks; trim ends from chicken. Cut each roll of chicken into 10 slices. Spread mayonnaise onto toast; top with chicken and thyme.
Makes 32.

▦ Recipe can be prepared 2 days ahead.
▦ Storage: Toasts, in airtight container. Chicken, covered, in refrigerator.
▦ Freeze: Not suitable.
▦ Microwave: Not suitable.

PEPPERED SMOKED CHEESE ROUNDS

250g packet cream cheese
2 cups (240g) coarsely grated smoked cheese
¼ cup (60ml) mango chutney
2 tablespoons finely chopped chives
¼ cup (35g) sesame seeds, toasted
¼ cup seasoned pepper
50 rice crackers
1 green shallot, finely sliced

Beat cream cheese in small bowl with electric mixer until smooth. Stir in smoked cheese, chutney and chives; cover, refrigerate 1 hour. Divide cheese mixture into 3 portions; shape each portion into a 20cm log by rolling in baking paper, cover; refrigerate 1 hour.

PASTRAMI MUFFINS WITH CHUTNEY MAYONNAISE

20g butter
4 green shallots, finely chopped
150g pastrami, finely chopped
1 cup (150g) self-raising flour
2 tablespoons caster sugar
1/4 cup chopped fresh basil
1/3 cup (25g) grated
  parmesan cheese
1 egg, lightly beaten
1 cup (250ml) milk
1/4 cup (20g) grated parmesan
  cheese, extra
1/3 cup (80ml) mango chutney
11/2 tablespoons mayonnaise

Heat butter in pan, add shallots and pastrami, cook, stirring, until shallots are soft; cool. Sift flour and sugar into bowl, stir in shallot mixture, basil, cheese, egg and milk, mix until just combined; do not over-mix. Spoon mixture into greased 3 x 12 hole mini muffin pans (1 tablespoon capacity); sprinkle with extra cheese. Bake in hot oven about 15 minutes. Serve muffins with combined chutney and mayonnaise.
Makes about 36.

▓ Recipe can be made a day ahead.
▓ Storage: Airtight container.
▓ Freeze: Suitable.
▓ Microwave: Not suitable.

LEFT: From back: Peppered Smoked Cheese Rounds; Chicken and Prosciutto Roulade Toasts.
BELOW: Pastrami Muffins with Chutney Mayonnaise.

Left: Plates and serviettes from The Bay Tree Kitchen Shop. Below: Basket and serviettes from Storehouse.

Roll each log in combined seeds and pepper, cover; refrigerate 1 hour or until firm. Trim ends from logs, cut into 1cm slices. Serve cheese rounds on rice crackers, top with shallot.
Makes about 50.

▓ Recipe can be prepared
  a week ahead.
▓ Storage: Cheese logs, covered,
  in refrigerator.
▓ Freeze: Not suitable.
▓ Microwave: Not suitable.

Chutneys, Jams and Relishes

The chutneys on these pages will keep in a cool, dark place up to a year, if jars are correctly sterilised and sealed. The relishes, jam and marmalade will keep for 2 months in the refrigerator. None of these recipes is suitable to freeze or microwave.

CHILLI JAM

2 tablespoons olive oil
2 large (700g) red peppers, chopped
2 cloves garlic, crushed
2 medium (300g) onions, chopped
3 small fresh red chillies, chopped
1/2 cup (125ml) white vinegar
1/2 cup (110g) caster sugar
1/4 cup (50g) brown sugar

Heat oil in large pan, add peppers, garlic, onions and chillies, cook, stirring, over low heat about 20 minutes or until peppers are soft. Add vinegar and caster sugar, stir over heat, without boiling, until sugar is dissolved. Simmer, uncovered, about 15 minutes or until mixture is thick. Stir in brown sugar; process mixture until finely chopped. Spoon into hot sterilised jars; seal while hot.
Makes about 1 1/2 cups (375ml).

ONION MARMALADE

4 large (1.2kg) red Spanish
    onions, sliced
1 1/2 cups (375ml) water
1/2 cup (125ml) brown malt vinegar
2/3 cup (130g) firmly packed
    brown sugar
2 teaspoons grated orange rind
1/2 cup (125ml) orange juice

Combine onions and water in large pan, boil, uncovered, stirring occasionally, about 20 minutes or until onions are soft and liquid evaporated. Add remaining ingredients, stir over heat, without boiling, until sugar is dissolved. Simmer, covered, 30 minutes. Remove cover, simmer, stirring occasionally, further 30 minutes or until mixture thickens. Spoon marmalade into hot sterilised jars; seal while hot.
Makes about 2 cups (500ml).

PINEAPPLE MINT RELISH

1 large (2kg) pineapple, peeled,
    cored, chopped
1 medium (150g) onion, chopped
2 cloves garlic, crushed
1 small fresh red chilli, chopped
2 teaspoons grated fresh ginger
1 cup (250ml) cider vinegar
1 cup (220g) sugar
1/4 cup chopped fresh mint

Combine all ingredients in large pan, stir over heat, without boiling, until sugar is dissolved. Simmer, uncovered, about 1 hour or until liquid has evaporated. Process half the mixture until pureed; combine with remaining mixture. Spoon into hot sterilised jars; seal while hot.
Makes about 2 cups (500ml).

ROASTED RED AND YELLOW PEPPER RELISH

2 large (700g) red peppers
2 large (700g) yellow peppers
2 cups (500ml) water
1 cup (250ml) white vinegar
1 cup (200g) firmly packed
    brown sugar
2 medium (300g) onions,
    finely chopped
1 small fresh red chilli, chopped
2 teaspoons dry mustard
1 tablespoon cornflour
2 tablespoons water, extra

Quarter peppers, remove seeds and membranes. Grill peppers, skin side up, until skin blisters and blackens. Peel away skin, chop peppers into 1cm pieces. Combine peppers with water, vinegar, sugar, onions, chilli and mustard in large pan, stir over heat, without boiling, until sugar is dissolved. Boil, uncovered, stirring occasionally, about 30 minutes or until mixture is reduced to about half. Stir in blended cornflour and extra water, stir over heat until mixture boils and thickens. Spoon relish into hot sterilised jars; seal while hot.
Makes about 2 1/2 cups (625ml).

INDIAN GREEN MANGO CHUTNEY

4 medium (1.5kg) green mangoes,
    peeled, chopped
1 tablespoon coarse cooking salt
1 tablespoon peanut oil
1 teaspoon dried crushed chillies
2 medium (300g) onions, chopped
2 cloves garlic, crushed
1 tablespoon grated fresh ginger
2 teaspoons coriander seeds
1 teaspoon cumin seeds
2 1/2 cups (625ml) white wine vinegar
2 cups (440g) sugar

Place mangoes and salt in large bowl, add enough cold water to just cover mangoes, cover; stand overnight.
  Drain mangoes; discard liquid. Heat oil in large pan, add chilli, onions, garlic, ginger and seeds, cook, stirring, until onions are soft. Add mangoes, vinegar and sugar, stir over heat, without boiling, until sugar is dissolved. Simmer, uncovered, about 1 1/2 hours or until mixture thickens. Spoon chutney into hot sterilised jars; seal while hot.
Makes about 4 cups (1 litre).

DRIED APRICOT, PEAR AND APPLE CHUTNEY

3 cups (450g) chopped dried pears
1 cup (90g) chopped dried apples
2 cups (300g) chopped dried apricots
1 litre (4 cups) boiling water
2 cups (500ml) brown malt vinegar
2 cups (400g) firmly packed
    brown sugar
1/4 teaspoon cayenne pepper
1 clove garlic, crushed
2 teaspoons brown mustard seeds
1/2 teaspoon ground nutmeg

Combine fruit and water in large heat-proof bowl, cover; stand 1 hour. Combine undrained fruit mixture in large pan with remaining ingredients, stir over heat, without boiling, until sugar is dissolved. Simmer, uncovered, stirring occasionally, about 1 hour or until mixture thickens. Spoon chutney into hot sterilised jars; seal while hot.
Makes about 6 cups (1.5 litres).

PEPPERED PLUM AND LEMON CHUTNEY

60g butter
2 medium (300g) onions, chopped
2 cloves garlic, crushed
2 teaspoons seasoned pepper
2 teaspoons grated fresh ginger
2 teaspoons brown mustard seeds
10 medium (1kg) blood plums,
   seeded, chopped
2 large (500g) tomatoes,
   peeled, chopped
1 tablespoon grated lemon rind
2 cups (400g) firmly packed
   brown sugar
2½ cups (625ml) brown malt vinegar

Melt butter in large pan, add onions, garlic, pepper, ginger and seeds, cook, stirring, until fragrant. Add remaining ingredients, stir over heat, without boiling, until sugar is dissolved. Simmer, uncovered, about 1¼ hours or until mixture thickens. Spoon chutney into hot sterilised jars; seal while hot.
Makes about 3 cups (750ml).

CITRUS BEETROOT CHUTNEY

10 medium (1.6kg) beetroot,
   peeled, grated
1 large (200g) onion, finely chopped
2 medium (360g) oranges,
   peeled, chopped
1½ cups (330g) caster sugar
2 teaspoons grated lemon rind
2 cups (500ml) white vinegar
2 teaspoons caraway seeds
½ cup (85g) chopped raisins

Combine beetroot, onion, oranges, sugar, rind, vinegar and seeds in large pan, stir over heat, without boiling, until sugar is dissolved. Simmer, uncovered, stirring occasionally, about 1 hour or

until mixture thickens. Process half the beetroot mixture until finely chopped; combine with remaining beetroot and raisins. Spoon chutney into hot sterilised jars; seal while hot.
Makes about 7 cups (1.75 litres).

1. Roasted Red and Yellow Pepper Relish
2. Indian Green Mango Chutney 3. Onion Marmalade 4. Chilli Jam 5. Dried Apricot, Pear and Apple Chutney 6. Pineapple Mint Relish 7. Citrus Beetroot Chutney
8. Peppered Plum and Lemon Chutney.

Stand from House; tray and cloth from Home & Garden on the Mall.

BUTTERMILK DAMPERS WITH PROSCIUTTO

2 medium (400g) red peppers
10 slices (150g) prosciutto
3 cups (450g) self-raising flour
2 small (140g) carrots, finely grated
2 tablespoons chopped fresh
**   coriander leaves**
1 cup (250ml) buttermilk
1/3 cup (80ml) water, approximately
1/2 cup (40g) finely grated
**   parmesan cheese**
350g baked ricotta cheese,
**   thinly sliced**
fresh coriander leaves, extra

Quarter peppers, remove seeds and membranes. Grill peppers, skin side up, until skin blisters and blackens. Peel away skin, chop peppers into 3cm pieces. Grill prosciutto until crisp, cool. Break into small pieces.

Sift flour into bowl, stir in carrots and coriander. Stir in buttermilk and enough water to mix to a soft, sticky dough. Turn dough onto floured surface; using floured hands, roll tablespoons of mixture into balls. Place balls about 3cm apart on greased oven trays, flatten to 4.5cm rounds; sprinkle with parmesan. Bake in moderately hot oven about 15 minutes or until dampers are puffed and browned; cool. Split dampers almost in half, leaving base and top intact. Fill with ricotta, prosciutto, pepper and extra coriander.
Makes about 40.

- Peppers and prosciutto can be prepared a day ahead.
- Storage: Covered, separately, in refrigerator.
- Freeze: Cooked dampers suitable.
- Microwave: Not suitable.

NORI ROLLS WITH DIPPING SAUCE

2 cups (400g) short-grain rice
2 cups (500ml) water
1/4 cup (60ml) rice vinegar
2 tablespoons sugar
1 teaspoon salt

BEEF AND BASIL VARIATION
1 large (500g) eggplant
1/3 cup (80ml) olive oil
2 medium (400g) red peppers
100g sliced rare roast beef
5 sheets sushi nori
1 cup loosely packed fresh
**   basil leaves**

SMOKED SALMON VARIATION
1 teaspoon vegetable oil
1 egg, lightly beaten
5 sheets sushi nori
1/2 medium (125g) avocado
2 teaspoons lemon juice
1 1/2 tablespoons sesame
**   seeds, toasted**
75g sliced smoked salmon

DIPPING SAUCE
2 egg yolks
1 teaspoon Dijon mustard
1 1/2 cups (375ml) light olive oil
2 tablespoons lemon juice
1/4 cup finely shredded fresh basil

Place rice and water in pan, simmer, covered, about 12 minutes or until rice is just tender. Remove from heat; stand, covered, 5 minutes. Transfer rice to large non-metallic bowl, gradually add combined vinegar, sugar and salt as you toss the rice with a spatula. At the same time, you will need help to fan rice so that it cools rapidly and becomes glossy.
Beef and Basil Variation: You will need 1 quantity of rice mixture. Cut eggplant lengthways into 5mm slices, brush all over with oil; grill until browned on both sides; cool. Quarter peppers, remove

seeds and membranes. Grill peppers, skin side up, until skin blisters and blackens. Peel away skin, cut into 1cm slices. Slice beef into 1cm strips.

Place a sheet of nori, rough side up, with long side towards you, on damp bamboo sushi mat. Place a fifth of the eggplant over nori in single layer. Spread a fifth of the rice mixture over nori, using wet fingers, pressing down firmly, leaving 4cm strip on far side. Place a fifth of the pepper, beef and basil across centre of rice. Starting at the edge closest to you, use bamboo mat to help roll the nori, pressing down firmly as you roll. Remove bamboo mat, use a sharp knife to trim ends, cut nori roll into 8 pieces. Repeat with remaining ingredients. Serve with dipping sauce.

Smoked Salmon Variation: You will need 1 quantity of rice mixture. Heat 22cm non-stick pan, add oil, pour in egg; cook, without stirring, until set. Remove omelette, cut into 2cm strips. Cut avocado into thin strips, brush with juice.

Follow instructions for Beef and Basil Variation, but sprinkle sesame seeds over rice, top with salmon, avocado and omelette across centre of rice.

Dipping Sauce: Blend or process egg yolks and mustard until smooth. Add oil gradually in a thin stream while motor is operating, blend until thick. Stir in juice, basil and enough water to make a thin consistency.

Makes 40 of each variation.

- ▓ Unsliced nori rolls and dipping sauce can be made a day ahead.
- ▓ Storage: Covered, separately, in refrigerator.
- ▓ Freeze: Not suitable.
- ▓ Microwave: Not suitable.

LEFT: Buttermilk Dampers with Prosciutto.
RIGHT: Nori Rolls with Dipping Sauce.

Left: China from Villeroy & Boch.

Canapes

Rice crackers, mini rice cakes, water crackers and toasted bread rounds are just some of the bases suitable for canapes. We used bread rounds cut from sliced white bread, brushed with butter, then toasted on oven trays in a moderate oven about 10 minutes. Any variety of bread can be used; rounds can be made 3 days ahead and stored in airtight containers. Canapes are best assembled just before serving. Recipes unsuitable to freeze or microwave.

Spread bases with:

1. Wasabi and mayonnaise; top with sliced rare-cooked tuna, finely sliced radishes and snow pea sprouts.

2. Goats' cheese; top with cooked sliced beetroot, chives and toasted pine nuts.

3. Sour cream; top with smoked salmon, avocado, baby capers and chervil leaves.

4. Olive paste; top with baked ricotta cheese, roasted egg tomato, quartered baby artichoke hearts and rosemary sprigs.

5. Plum sauce; top with sliced Chinese barbecued pork, quartered canned baby corn spears and sliced green shallots.

6. Pesto; top with oil-brushed grilled or roasted zucchini, eggplant and red peppers, then fresh basil leaves.

7. Mascarpone cheese; top with sliced figs, sliced prosciutto and sage leaves.

8. Mayonnaise; top with small cooked prawns, cooked fresh asparagus tips, lemon slices and dill sprigs.

9. Mayonnaise; top with torn pieces of radicchio leaves, sliced carambola (star fruit), blue vein cheese and coriander leaves.

10. Horseradish cream; top with fanned gherkins, slices of pastrami and sliced fresh red chillies.

HOT SAVOURIES

Add pizzazz to any party or special occasion with the fabulous flavour combinations presented here. Some can be prepared or made ahead and reheated, while others are cooked just before serving. Mixing cold and hot savouries is a clever idea, because, while the cold ones are going round, you have time to reheat or cook the hot ones. Plan ahead, go for a variety of tastes, colours and textures, and you're set for success.

PESTO SALAMI ROLLS

18 slices white bread
200g mild salami, chopped
¼ cup (30g) seedless black olives, chopped
⅓ cup sun-dried tomatoes in oil, drained, chopped
⅓ cup (25g) grated parmesan cheese
2 tablespoons mayonnaise
2 tablespoons chopped fresh parsley
¼ cup (60ml) bottled pesto
½ small (75g) red pepper, finely chopped
40g butter, melted

Cut crusts from bread, roll out bread slices until 2mm thick. Add salami to hot pan, cook, stirring, until salami is almost crisp; drain on absorbent paper; cool. Blend or process salami, olives, tomatoes, cheese, mayonnaise, parsley, pesto and pepper until just combined. Spread 1 tablespoon salami mixture onto each slice of bread, roll up. Cut rolls in half, secure each half with a toothpick. Place rolls on oven trays, brush with butter. Bake in moderate oven about 10 minutes or until browned. Makes 36.

▩ Recipe can be prepared a day ahead.
▩ Storage: Covered, in refrigerator.
▩ Freeze: Uncooked rolls suitable.
▩ Microwave: Not suitable.
▩ Reheat: Place cooked rolls on oven trays in hot oven about 5 minutes.

BASIL AND BLUE CHEESE TARTS

30g butter
2 green shallots, chopped
1½ tablespoons plain flour
⅔ cup (160ml) milk
¼ teaspoon ground nutmeg
150g blue vein cheese
1 teaspoon olive oil
80g mushrooms, finely chopped
1 bacon rasher, finely chopped
1 tablespoon chopped fresh basil
1 cup (70g) stale breadcrumbs
4 x 50g packets of 12 savoury tartlet cases
roasted red pepper strips

Melt butter in pan, add shallots, cook, stirring, until shallots are soft. Add flour, stir over heat until bubbling. Remove from heat, gradually stir in milk; return to heat, stir until mixture boils and thickens. Remove from heat, stir in nutmeg and cheese.

Heat oil in pan, add mushrooms and bacon, cook, stirring, until mushrooms are soft; stir in basil, breadcrumbs and cheese mixture.

Place tartlet cases on oven trays; fill with mushroom mixture. Bake tarts in moderate oven about 10 minutes or until heated through. Top with strips of roasted red pepper.
Makes 48.

▩ Cheese mixture can be made a day ahead.
▩ Storage: Covered, in refrigerator.
▩ Freeze: Not suitable.
▩ Microwave: Cheese mixture suitable.
▩ Reheat: Place cheese mixture in pan over low heat until warmed through.

CHORIZO CHEESE PUFFS

1 cup (150g) self-raising flour
½ cup (125ml) water
2 eggs, lightly beaten
300g chorizo sausage, finely chopped
1 small (150g) red pepper, finely chopped
½ cup (40g) finely grated parmesan cheese
3 cloves garlic, crushed
¼ cup chopped fresh chives
2 teaspoons ground cumin
vegetable oil for deep-frying

Sift flour into medium bowl, stir in water, eggs, sausage, pepper, cheese, garlic, chives and cumin. Drop tablespoons of mixture into hot oil in batches, cook until browned; drain on absorbent paper. Makes about 40.

▩ Recipe best made just before serving.
▩ Freeze: Not suitable.
▩ Microwave: Not suitable.

From back: Chorizo Cheese Puffs; Pesto Salami Rolls; Basil and Blue Cheese Tarts.

HAM AND EGG-FILLED MUSHROOMS

1 teaspoon butter
1 clove garlic, crushed
1/2 cup (100g) finely chopped ham
2 tablespoons chopped
fresh chives
2 eggs, lightly beaten
2 tablespoons cream
30 medium (about 550g) button
mushrooms

Melt butter in pan, add garlic, ham and chives; cook, stirring, a few minutes. Pour in combined eggs and cream; cook gently over low heat, stirring occasionally, until just set.

Remove stems from mushrooms. Place mushrooms on oven trays, fill with egg mixture; bake in moderately hot oven about 5 minutes or until mushrooms are hot.
Makes 30.

▓ Recipe best made just before serving.
▓ Freeze: Not suitable.
▓ Microwave: Not suitable.

ZUCCHINI, LEEK AND FETA FRITTATA

1 tablespoon olive oil
20g butter
2 medium (240g) zucchini,
coarsely grated
2 small (400g) leeks, sliced
1 clove garlic, crushed
8 eggs, lightly beaten
1/2 cup (125ml) cream
100g feta cheese, crumbled
1/2 cup (40g) grated parmesan cheese
2 tablespoons chopped fresh mint
2 tablespoons polenta
2 tablespoons grated parmesan
cheese, extra
50g feta cheese, crumbled, extra

Grease 23cm square slab pan, cover base with foil. Heat oil and butter in frying pan, add zucchini, leeks and garlic, cook, stirring, 3 minutes, cover, cook until leeks are soft; cool.

Combine leek mixture with eggs, cream, cheeses and mint in bowl; pour into prepared pan. Sprinkle with combined polenta and extra cheeses. Bake in moderate oven about 40 minutes or until set. Cool in pan.

Cut frittata into 25 squares, cut each square in half diagonally.
Makes 50.

▓ Recipe can be made a day ahead.
▓ Storage: Covered, in refrigerator.
▓ Freeze: Not suitable.
▓ Microwave: Not suitable.
▓ Reheat: Place frittata on oven trays
  in hot oven about 10 minutes.

NACHOS BITES

230g packet plain corn chips
1 cup (270g) canned refried beans
1/4 cup (60ml) sour cream
1 tablespoon chopped fresh
coriander leaves
2 teaspoons Cajun seasoning
1 cup (125g) grated tasty
cheddar cheese
2 medium (260g) tomatoes,
finely sliced
1 small (190g) avocado,
finely chopped
2 tablespoons finely chopped
flat-leaf parsley

Select 60 large, unbroken chips, place in single layer on lightly greased oven trays. Top chips with combined beans, cream, coriander and seasoning; sprinkle with cheese.

Just before serving, bake in moderately hot oven about 8 minutes or until cheese is melted and chips crisp. Top each chip with tomato and avocado; sprinkle with parsley.
Makes 60.

▓ Bean mixture can be made
  a day ahead.
▓ Storage: Covered, in refrigerator.
▓ Freeze: Not suitable.
▓ Microwave: Not suitable.

LEFT: From back: Zucchini, Leek and Feta Frittata; Ham and Egg-Filled Mushrooms. BELOW: Nachos Bites.

Left: China from Accoutrement. Below: Plate from Accoutrement; cloth from Art House.

Vol-au-vent Variations

A long-time favourite finger food, the vol-au-vent is truly a light-as-air taste sensation. Here we give you a few traditional fillings and several innovative, scrumptious ones. Each filling makes enough to fill 36 oyster cases; you will need 3 x 60g packets of 12 oyster cases. All fillings, except the souffle bacon and chives, can be made a day ahead and stored, covered, in the refrigerator. Oyster cases can be filled 1 hour ahead and stored, covered, in the refrigerator. To heat, place vol-au-vents on oven tray in moderate oven for about 10 minutes. None of these recipes is suitable to freeze, and only the basic filling recipe is suitable to microwave.

BASIC FILLING

60g butter
½ small (40g) onion, finely chopped
¼ cup (35g) plain flour
1 cup (250ml) milk

Melt butter in pan, add onion, cook, stirring, until onion is soft. Stir in flour, stir over heat until mixture is dry and grainy. Remove from heat, gradually stir in milk; return to heat, stir until mixture boils and thickens.
Makes about 1½ cups (375ml).

SALMON AND CHEESE

105g can red salmon, drained, flaked
½ quantity basic filling
½ cup (60g) grated tasty
    cheddar cheese
1 tablespoon chopped fresh parsley
thin lemon wedges
finely chopped green shallot

Combine salmon, basic filling, cheese and parsley in bowl; divide among cases. Heat as directed above; top with lemon and shallot.

BLUE CHEESE AND CHIVES

½ quantity basic filling
150g blue vein cheese, crumbled
⅔ cup (80g) grated tasty
    cheddar cheese
⅓ cup cooked rice
1 tablespoon chopped fresh chives
chopped fresh chives, extra

Combine basic filling, cheeses, rice and chives in bowl; divide among cases. Heat as directed above; top with extra chives.

CURRIED CRAB

½ quantity basic filling
2 x 170g cans crab meat, drained
3 teaspoons mild curry powder
¼ teaspoon ground cumin
1 tablespoon chopped fresh parsley
fresh parsley, extra

Combine basic filling, crab, spices and parsley in bowl; divide among cases. Heat as directed above; top with extra parsley.

SATAY LAMB

Make basic filling using 1 cup (250ml) coconut milk instead of milk.

1 teaspoon vegetable oil
3 (240g) lamb fillets, finely chopped
½ quantity basic filling
½ cup (125ml) satay sauce
½ teaspoon chopped fresh thyme
finely chopped yellow pepper
fresh basil leaves

Heat oil in pan, add lamb, cook, stirring, until well browned, stir in basic filling, sauce and thyme; divide among cases. Heat as directed above; top with pepper and basil.

HAM AND CORN

½ quantity basic filling
3 slices (60g) ham, finely chopped
130g can creamed corn
½ cup (60g) grated tasty
    cheddar cheese
1 tablespoon chopped fresh parsley
chopped fresh parsley, extra

Combine basic filling, ham, corn, cheese and parsley in bowl; divide among cases. Heat as directed above; sprinkle with extra parsley.

SOUFFLE BACON AND CHIVES

6 bacon rashers, finely chopped
½ quantity basic filling
½ cup (40g) grated parmesan cheese
2 tablespoons chopped fresh chives
2 teaspoons chopped fresh oregano
2 egg whites

Heat pan, add bacon, cook, stirring, until bacon is crisp; drain. Reserve 1 tablespoon of the bacon. Combine remaining bacon, basic filling, cheese, half the chives and oregano in bowl.
  Just before serving, beat egg whites in small bowl until soft peaks form, fold into bacon mixture; divide among cases. Bake as directed above; top with reserved bacon and chives.

THAI CHICKEN

½ quantity basic filling
1 cup (200g) finely chopped
    cooked chicken
2 teaspoons Thai red curry paste
2 teaspoons chopped fresh
    coriander leaves
thin strips yellow pepper
thinly sliced small fresh red chilli
flat-leaf parsley leaves

Combine basic filling, chicken, paste and coriander in bowl; divide among cases. Heat as directed above; top with pepper, chilli and parsley.

SMOKED COD AND DILL

300g smoked cod
½ quantity basic filling
¼ cup (30g) grated tasty
    cheddar cheese
2 teaspoons chopped fresh dill
fresh dill sprigs, extra

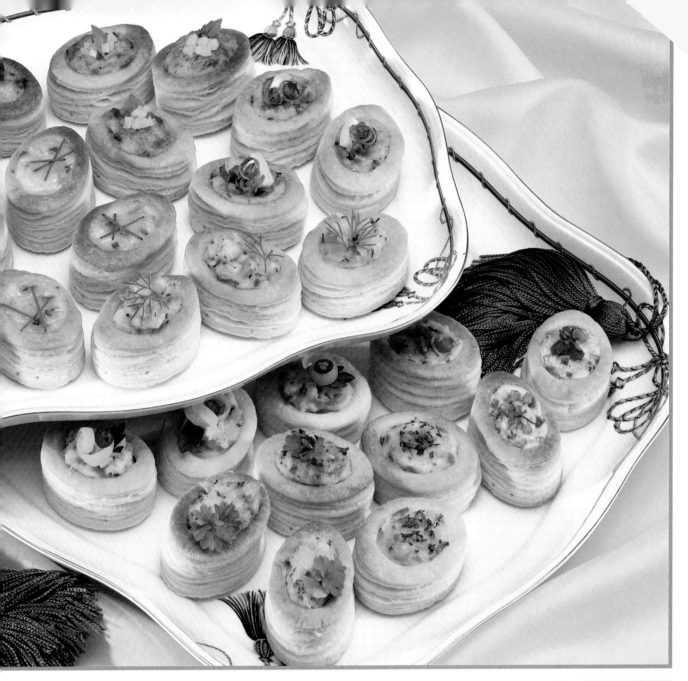

Poach, steam or microwave fish until tender; drain. Remove skin and bones, flake fish. Combine fish with basic filling, cheese and dill; divide among cases. Heat as directed above; top with extra dill.

MEXICAN

½ quantity basic filling
1 large (250g) tomato, peeled seeded, finely chopped
130g can corn kernels, drained
¼ cup canned red kidney beans, rinsed, drained, chopped
⅓ cup (40g) grated tasty cheddar cheese
2 teaspoons chopped fresh coriander
½ teaspoon chilli powder
½ teaspoon ground cumin
thin strips red pepper

Combine basic filling, tomato, corn, beans, cheese, coriander and spices in bowl; divide among cases. Heat as directed above; top with red pepper.

CHICKEN AND ASPARAGUS

½ bunch (125g) asparagus, finely chopped
½ quantity basic filling
½ cup (100g) finely chopped cooked chicken
½ cup (60g) grated tasty cheddar cheese
1 tablespoon chopped fresh basil
finely chopped green shallot
finely chopped red pepper

Boil, steam or microwave asparagus until just tender; drain. Combine asparagus with basic filling, chicken, cheese and basil in bowl; divide among cases. Heat as directed above; top with shallot and pepper.

1. Mexican 2. Satay Lamb 3. Salmon and Cheese 4. Smoked Cod and Dill 5. Blue Cheese and Chives 6. Chicken and Asparagus 7. Thai Chicken 8. Curried Crab 9. Ham and Corn 10. Souffle Bacon and Chives.

China from Villeroy & Boch; tassels from Home & Garden on the Mall.

CY CHICKEN PARCELS H SATAY SAUCE

aspoons olive oil
 mall (80g) onion, finely chopped
1 clove garlic, crushed
1 teaspoon ground cumin
1 tablespoon curry paste
1 cup (200g) finely chopped
   cooked chicken
1 tablespoon chopped fresh
   coriander leaves
½ cup (125ml) low-fat sour cream
4 sheets ready-rolled puff pastry
1 egg, lightly beaten

SATAY SAUCE
½ cup (130g) smooth
   peanut butter
⅓ cup (80ml) mild sweet chilli sauce
¾ cup (180ml) chicken stock
1 tablespoon lemon juice
1 tablespoon chopped fresh
   coriander leaves

Heat oil in pan, add onion and garlic, cook, stirring, until onion is soft. Add cumin and paste, cook, stirring, until fragrant, stir in chicken, coriander and sour cream; cool.

Cut each pastry sheet into 4 strips, cut each strip crossways to give 3 rectangles. Place 1 teaspoon of mixture in centre of each pastry rectangle, lightly brush edges with egg, fold in long sides, fold over ends, to enclose filling. Place parcels, seam side down, about 3cm apart on greased oven trays, brush with egg. Bake in moderately hot oven about 20 minutes or until browned. Serve with satay sauce.

Satay Sauce: Place all ingredients in medium pan, stir over heat until hot.

Makes 48.

- Parcels and sauce can be made a day ahead.
- Storage: Covered, separately, in refrigerator.
- Freeze: Uncooked parcels suitable.
- Microwave: Not suitable.
- Reheat: Place parcels on oven trays in hot oven 5 minutes.

SEAFOOD FRITTERS WITH GARLIC CHILLI MAYONNAISE

1 cup (150g) self-raising flour
½ cup (125ml) beer
2 eggs, lightly beaten
500g medium uncooked prawns, shelled, chopped
200g scallops, chopped
6 oysters, chopped
2 green shallots, finely chopped
2 tablespoons chopped fresh coriander leaves
1 teaspoon grated lime rind
½ teaspoon sambal oelek
vegetable oil for deep-frying

GARLIC CHILLI MAYONNAISE
1 egg
2 cloves garlic, crushed
1 teaspoon sambal oelek
1 tablespoon lime juice
1 cup (250ml) light olive oil

Sift flour into bowl, whisk in beer and eggs; stir in seafood, shallots, coriander, rind and sambal oelek. Just before serving, drop tablespoons of mixture in batches into hot oil, deep-fry until browned and cooked through; drain on absorbent paper. Serve with garlic chilli mayonnaise.
Garlic Chilli Mayonnaise: Process egg, garlic, sambal oelek and juice until smooth. With motor operating, add oil in a thin stream, process until mixture has thickened.
Makes about 35.

- Fritters best made just before serving. Garlic chilli mayonnaise can be made 2 days ahead.
- Storage: Covered, in refrigerator.
- Freeze: Not suitable.
- Microwave: Not suitable.

TEMPURA OYSTERS WITH RED PEPPER DRESSING

1 sheet sushi nori
24 oysters in shells
cornflour
vegetable oil for deep-frying

TEMPURA BATTER
1 cup (150g) cornflour
½ cup (125ml) iced water
1 egg yolk

RED PEPPER DRESSING
1 small (150g) red pepper
2 teaspoons mirin
1 teaspoon soy sauce
¼ teaspoon sambal oelek

Finely slice about quarter of the sheet of nori. Remove oysters from shells; drain on absorbent paper. Wash and reserve shells, place on oven tray, heat in slow oven about 10 minutes. Toss oysters in cornflour, shake away excess. Dip oysters in tempura batter. Deep-fry oysters in hot oil in batches until lightly browned; drain on absorbent paper. Serve oysters in shells, topped with red pepper dressing and nori.
Tempura Batter: Sift cornflour into bowl, whisk in combined water and egg yolk.
Red Pepper Dressing: Quarter pepper, remove seeds and membranes; grill pepper, skin side up, until skin blisters and blackens; peel away skin. Blend or process pepper with remaining ingredients until smooth.
Makes 24.

- Recipe best made just before serving. Dressing can be made a day ahead.
- Storage: Covered, in refrigerator.
- Freeze: Not suitable.
- Microwave: Not suitable.

LEFT: From back: Spicy Chicken Parcels with Satay Sauce; Seafood Fritters with Garlic Chilli Mayonnaise.
BELOW: Tempura Oysters with Red Pepper Dressing.

Below: China from Waterford Wedgwood; oyster forks from The Bay Tree Kitchen Shop.

MEXICAN PROFITEROLES

40g butter
½ cup (125ml) water
½ cup (75g) plain flour
½ teaspoon chilli powder
2 eggs
2 tablespoons chopped fresh chives

FILLING
1 tablespoon olive oil
1 small (80g) onion, finely chopped
2 cloves garlic, crushed
1 small (150g) red pepper,
** finely chopped**
2 tablespoons taco seasoning mix
2 teaspoons ground cumin
¼ cup (35g) plain flour
1 cup (250ml) milk
½ cup (60g) grated tasty
** cheddar cheese**
2 tablespoons sour cream

Combine butter and water in pan, stir over heat until butter has melted and mixture boils. Add flour and chilli powder all at once, stir vigorously over heat until mixture leaves side of pan. Transfer mixture to small bowl, add eggs 1 at a time, beat with electric mixer on low speed until smooth; stir in chives. Drop teaspoons of mixture about 5cm apart on ungreased oven trays. Bake in moderately hot oven 10 minutes, reduce heat to moderate, bake about further 10 minutes or until profiteroles are crisp. Cut profiteroles in half, place 1 teaspoon filling in each half, rejoin halves.
Filling: Heat oil in pan, add onion, garlic and pepper, cook, stirring, until pepper is soft. Add seasoning, cumin and flour, stir over heat until mixture is dry and grainy. Remove from heat, gradually stir in milk, return to heat, stir until mixture boils and thickens; cool 5 minutes. Stir in cheese and cream.
Makes about 50.

■ Profiteroles and filling can be made a day ahead.
■ Storage: Profiteroles, in airtight container. Filling, covered, in refrigerator.
■ Freeze: Unfilled profiteroles suitable.
■ Microwave: Filling suitable.
■ Reheat: Place filling in pan, stir over heat until hot.

SPICY BEEF AND CARAMELISED ONION TARTS

50g butter
1 tablespoon olive oil
2 medium (300g) onions, sliced
2 teaspoons chopped fresh thyme
150g beef eye-fillet, thinly sliced
¼ teaspoon cayenne pepper
3 x 50g packets of 12 savoury
** tartlet cases**

Heat butter and oil in pan, add onions and thyme, cook gently, stirring occasionally, until onions are soft and browned; cool 5 minutes. Combine beef, pepper and onion mixture in bowl, place tartlet cases on oven tray, divide beef mixture among cases. Just before serving, bake in moderate oven about 10 minutes or until beef is cooked.
Makes 36.

■ Beef mixture can be made 3 hours ahead.
■ Storage: Covered, in refrigerator.
■ Freeze: Not suitable.
■ Microwave: Not suitable.

CHEESE AND BACON POTATOES

15 (600g) baby new potatoes,
** unpeeled**
120g camembert cheese,
** finely chopped**
2 tablespoons finely grated
** parmesan cheese**
2 bacon rashers, finely chopped
1 tablespoon chopped fresh sage
2 tablespoons packaged
** breadcrumbs**
¼ cup (20g) finely grated parmesan
** cheese, extra**

Boil, steam or microwave potatoes until just tender; drain, cool. Cut potatoes in half. Using a melon baller, scoop out about a third of potato flesh, mash flesh; reserve. Trim bases of potatoes so they sit flat. Combine reserved potato with cheeses, bacon, sage and breadcrumbs in bowl; spoon mixture into potato halves, sprinkle with extra cheese. Place on greased oven tray. Bake in moderately hot oven about 15 minutes or until heated through.
Makes 30.

■ Recipe best made just before serving.
■ Freeze: Not suitable.
■ Microwave: Potatoes suitable.
■ Reheat: Place potatoes on oven tray in hot oven about 5 minutes.

RIGHT: Mexican Profiteroles; Spicy Beef and Caramelised Onion Tarts.
BELOW: Cheese and Bacon Potatoes.

Right: Glass plate from Accoutrement; martini glass from Elvy Agencies. Below: Plate from Ventura Design.

MUSHROOM-TOPPED POLENTA TRIANGLES

1 litre (4 cups) chicken stock
20g butter
1¼ cups (210g) polenta
1 cup (80g) grated parmesan cheese
plain flour
vegetable oil for shallow-frying
⅓ cup (25g) flaked parmesan cheese

MUSHROOM TOPPING
50g butter
2 cloves garlic, crushed
2 bacon rashers, finely chopped
3 green shallots, finely chopped
300g flat mushrooms, thinly sliced

100g shiitake mushrooms, thinly sliced
100g enoki mushrooms, roughly chopped
3 teaspoons chopped fresh oregano
3 teaspoons chopped fresh thyme
1 tablespoon port

Grease 26cm x 32cm Swiss roll pan, cover base with baking paper. Bring stock and butter to boil in medium pan, gradually add polenta, simmer, stirring, about 15 minutes or until thick. Remove from heat, stir in grated parmesan. Spread polenta mixture into prepared pan, cover; refrigerate 1 hour or until firm.

Cut polenta into 30 x 5cm squares, cut each square in half diagonally. Toss polenta triangles in flour, shake away excess flour. Shallow-fry triangles in batches in hot oil until crisp; drain on absorbent paper.

Just before serving, place triangles on oven trays, spoon over mushroom topping, top with parmesan flakes. Bake in moderately hot oven about 10 minutes or until heated through.

Mushroom Topping: Heat butter in large pan, add remaining ingredients, cook, stirring, about 5 minutes or until liquid is evaporated.

SPICY SAUSAGE ROLLS

1 tablespoon olive oil
1 medium (150g) onion,
**   finely chopped**
2 cloves garlic, crushed
2 teaspoons fennel seeds, crushed
2 teaspoons crushed dried chillies
2 tablespoons chopped
**   fresh rosemary**
1/4 cup (60ml) tomato paste
1kg sausage mince
1 cup (70g) stale breadcrumbs
4 sheets ready-rolled puff pastry
1 egg yolk

ROASTED TOMATO SAUCE
8 large (720g) egg tomatoes, halved
1 teaspoon salt
freshly ground black pepper
1 teaspoon sugar
2 teaspoons chopped fresh rosemary
1/3 cup (80ml) olive oil

Heat oil in pan, add onion, garlic, seeds, chilli and rosemary, cook, stirring, until onion is soft; cool. Stir in paste, mince and crumbs.

Cut each pastry sheet into 3 even rectangles. Spoon sausage mixture into piping bag fitted with 1cm plain tube. Pipe a line of sausage mixture along centre of each rectangle. Brush edges of rectangles with egg yolk, roll over to enclose. Mark top of each roll in a criss-cross pattern, brush with more egg yolk. Place rolls, seam side down, on oven trays. Bake in hot oven about 20 minutes or until browned. Using a serrated knife, cut each roll into 6 pieces. Serve with roasted tomato sauce.

Roasted Tomato Sauce: Place tomatoes, cut side up, on oven tray, sprinkle with salt, pepper, sugar and rosemary, drizzle with half the oil. Bake in hot oven about 25 minutes or until tomatoes are very soft. Blend or process tomatoes until smooth; stir in remaining oil.
Makes 72.

◾ Recipe can be made a day ahead.
◾ Storage: Covered, separately,
    in refrigerator.
◾ Freeze: Roasted tomato sauce and
    uncooked rolls suitable.
◾ Microwave: Not suitable.
◾ Reheat: Place rolls on oven trays
    in hot oven about 5 minutes.

Makes 60.

◾ Polenta can be prepared a day
    ahead. Mushroom topping best
    made just before serving.
◾ Storage: Polenta, covered,
    in refrigerator.
◾ Freeze: Not suitable.
◾ Microwave: Not suitable.

ABOVE: Mushroom-Topped Polenta Triangles.
RIGHT: Spicy Sausage Rolls.

Above: China from Accoutrement; tray from Art House.
Right: China from The Bay Tree Kitchen Shop.

HERBED POTATO FRITTERS

2 medium (400g) potatoes, chopped
2 teaspoons olive oil
2 cloves garlic, crushed
1 bacon rasher, finely chopped
1 small (150g) red pepper,
    finely chopped
2 tablespoons chopped fresh chives
2 tablespoons chopped fresh basil
1 egg, lightly beaten
plain flour
1 egg, extra
2 tablespoons milk
½ cup (50g) packaged breadcrumbs
vegetable oil for deep-frying

DIPPING SAUCE
1 teaspoon vegetable oil
1 small (80g) onion, finely chopped
2 cloves garlic, crushed
2 tablespoons tomato paste
425g can tomatoes
1 tablespoon chopped fresh basil
1 small fresh red chilli, finely chopped

Boil, steam or microwave potatoes until tender, mash until smooth. Heat oil in pan, add garlic, bacon and pepper, cook, stirring, until bacon is crisp. Combine mashed potato, bacon mixture, herbs and egg in large bowl; refrigerate 2 hours. Drop rounded teaspoons of potato mixture into flour, shape into rounds, dip into combined extra egg and milk, then breadcrumbs. Just before serving, deep-fry potato fritters in hot oil in batches until browned; drain on absorbent paper. Serve with dipping sauce.

Dipping Sauce: Heat oil in pan, add onion and garlic, cook, stirring, until onion is soft. Add paste, undrained crushed tomatoes, basil and chilli, simmer, uncovered, about 10 minutes or until sauce has thickened slightly.

Makes about 50.

- ◼ Potato fritters can be prepared a day ahead. Dipping sauce can be made a day ahead.
- ◼ Storage: Covered, separately, in refrigerator.
- ◼ Freeze: Not suitable.
- ◼ Microwave: Potatoes suitable.

RIGHT: From left: Cornish Pasties;
Triple-Cheese Tarts.
BELOW: Herbed Potato Fritters.

Right: China from Opus Design; tray from Pacific East India Co. Below: Glass platter from Pacific East India Co.

TRIPLE-CHEESE TARTS

20 slices white bread
40g butter, melted
30g butter, extra
1 medium (150g) onion, finely chopped
1 bacon rasher, finely chopped
¼ cup (35g) plain flour
1 cup (250ml) milk
¼ cup (30g) finely grated tasty
    cheddar cheese
¼ cup (20g) grated parmesan cheese
25g blue vein cheese
2 tablespoons pine nuts, toasted
1 egg yolk
1 tablespoon chopped fresh parsley
snipped fresh chives

Cut crusts from bread, roll slices until 2mm thick, cut 2 x 5cm rounds from each slice, brush on both sides with melted butter. Press slices firmly into 40 holes of mini muffin pans (1 table-

spoon capacity). Bake in moderate oven about 7 minutes or until crisp.

Melt extra butter in pan, add onion and bacon, cook, stirring, until onion is soft. Add flour, stir over heat until mixture is dry and grainy. Remove from heat, gradually stir in milk, stir over heat until mixture boils and thickens. Remove from heat, stir in cheeses, nuts, egg yolk and parsley. Spoon cheese mixture into bread cases; sprinkle with chives.
Makes 40.

■ Bread cases and cheese mixture can be made 2 days ahead.
■ Storage: Bread cases, in airtight container. Cheese mixture, covered, in refrigerator.
■ Freeze: Not suitable.
■ Microwave: Cheese mixture suitable.
■ Reheat: Place tarts on oven trays in hot oven 5 minutes.

CORNISH PASTIES

2 teaspoons vegetable oil
100g beef rump steak, finely chopped
1 small (80g) onion, finely chopped
½ small (35g) carrot, finely chopped
½ small (60g) potato, finely chopped
¼ cup (30g) frozen peas
¼ cup (60ml) port
1 teaspoon cornflour
2 tablespoons water
½ teaspoon beef stock powder
**4 sheets ready-rolled
    shortcrust pastry**
2 egg yolks

Heat oil in pan, add beef, stir over high heat until browned. Add onion, carrot and potato, cook, stirring, until vegetables are tender. Add peas and port, stir in blended cornflour, water and stock powder, stir over heat until mixture boils and thickens; cool.

Cut 12 x 7cm rounds from each pastry sheet, place 1 teaspoon of beef mixture onto each round, brush edges with a little water, fold in half to enclose filling; pinch edges together. Place pasties upright on greased oven trays; brush with egg yolks. Bake in moderately hot oven about 20 minutes or until browned.
Makes 48.

■ Pasties can be made a day ahead.
■ Storage: Covered, in refrigerator.
■ Freeze: Cooked or uncooked pasties suitable.
■ Microwave: Not suitable.
■ Reheat: Place pasties on oven trays in hot oven 5 minutes.

Pizza Toppings

Making platters of these bite-sized pizzas is as easy as pie! The recipe for the pizza bases makes 32 bases that can be baked a week ahead and stored in airtight containers. Untopped, they are suitable to freeze, but not suitable to microwave. Each of the tasty toppings will cover 32 pizza bases; each can be made 1 day ahead and kept, covered, in the refrigerator. None is suitable to freeze or microwave. Pizzas can be assembled 2 hours ahead and stored, covered, in refrigerator. Pizzas best made just before serving.

PIZZA BASES

2 sheets ready-rolled butter puff pastry

Cut pastry into 16 x 5.5cm rounds, place on greased oven trays. Bake in very hot oven about 8 minutes or until browned; cool. Split pastry rounds in half, place, split side up, on oven trays. Spread with desired topping. Just before serving, bake, uncovered, in hot oven about 10 minutes.

SMOKED SALMON AND CAPERS

1 cup (200g) ricotta cheese
3 teaspoons hot water
2 tablespoons finely chopped fresh chives
3 teaspoons horseradish cream
6 slices (180g) smoked salmon, chopped
3 teaspoons drained tiny capers
fresh dill sprigs

Combine cheese and water in bowl; stir in chives and cream. Spread cheese mixture over heated pastry bases, top with salmon, capers and dill.

CAJUN PRAWN

600g uncooked medium prawns
1/2 cup (125ml) tomato pasta sauce
3 teaspoons Cajun seasoning
thin strips lemon rind

Shell and devein prawns; finely chop. Combine prawns, sauce and seasoning in bowl, cover; refrigerate 3 hours. Spoon prawn mixture onto bases. Bake as directed; top with rind.

BLUE CHEESE AND LEEK

2 teaspoons vegetable oil
1 small (200g) leek, sliced
2/3 cup (160ml) bottled tomato pasta sauce
90g blue vein cheese, crumbled

Heat oil in pan, add leek, cook, stirring, until soft. Spread bases with sauce, top with cheese, then leek mixture. Bake as directed.

SUN-DRIED TOMATO AND ARTICHOKE

1/2 cup (125ml) bottled tomato pasta sauce, strained
1/3 cup (80ml) sun-dried tomato paste
8 drained baby artichoke hearts, quartered
1/3 cup (25g) finely grated parmesan cheese
1 tablespoon chopped fresh parsley
parmesan cheese flakes, extra

Combine sauce and paste in bowl, spread over bases, top with artichokes, then cheese. Bake as directed; sprinkle with parsley and extra cheese.

ROASTED PEPPER AND OLIVES

3 medium (600g) yellow peppers
2/3 cup (160ml) bottled tomato pasta sauce
1/4 cup (30g) seedless black olives, sliced
40g goats' cheese
fresh basil leaves

Quarter peppers, remove seeds and membranes. Grill peppers, skin side up, until skin blisters and blackens. Peel away skin, slice peppers thinly. Spread bases with sauce, top with peppers, olives and cheese. Bake as directed; top with basil.

CHICKEN AND PESTO

2/3 cup (160ml) bottled pesto
3/4 cup (150g) finely chopped cooked chicken
1 1/2 tablespoons pine nuts
1/3 cup (25g) finely grated parmesan cheese
fresh basil leaves

Spread bases with pesto, top with chicken, nuts and cheese. Bake as directed; top with basil.

TANDOORI LAMB WITH YOGURT

4 (320g) lamb fillets
2 tablespoons plain yogurt
2 teaspoons tandoori paste
3 teaspoons chopped fresh
    coriander leaves
2/3 cup (160ml) bottled tomato
    pasta sauce
1/2 cup (125ml) plain yogurt, extra
1/2 small (65g) cucumber, peeled,
    seeded, chopped
fresh coriander leaves, extra

Combine lamb, yogurt, paste and coriander in bowl; cover, refrigerate 3 hours or overnight. Grill lamb until browned and tender; cool. Slice lamb thinly. Spread heated pastry bases with sauce, top with lamb, then extra yogurt, cucumber and extra coriander.

ITALIAN SAUSAGE AND MUSHROOM

3 teaspoons olive oil
12 (390g) small Italian sausages
1 medium (150g) onion,
    finely chopped
100g button mushrooms, sliced
2/3 cup (160ml) bottled tomato
    pasta sauce
1/3 cup (25g) finely grated
    parmesan cheese
finely grated parmesan cheese, extra
fresh coriander leaves

Heat 1 teaspoon of the oil in pan, add sausages, cook until browned all over; remove from pan. Heat remaining oil in same pan, add onion and mushrooms, cook, stirring, until onion is soft. Cut sausages into 5mm slices. Spread bases with sauce, top with sausages and onion mixture; sprinkle with cheese. Bake as directed; top with extra cheese and coriander leaves.

1. Prosciutto and Sage 2. Italian Sausage and Mushroom 3. Sun-Dried Tomato and Artichoke 4. Potato and Rosemary 5. Cajun Prawn 6. Tandoori Lamb with Yogurt 7. Roasted Eggplant and Bocconcini 8. Smoked Salmon and Capers 9. Roasted Pepper and Olives 10. Blue Cheese and Leek 11. Chicken and Pesto.

ROASTED EGGPLANT AND BOCCONCINI

3 (180g) finger eggplants
1½ tablespoons olive oil
3 teaspoons chopped fresh thyme
2/3 cup (160ml) bottled tomato
    pasta sauce
2 teaspoons olive paste
4 (40g) bocconcini cheese,
    thinly sliced
fresh thyme sprigs, extra

Cut eggplants into 32 x 5mm slices; brush both sides of each slice with oil, sprinkle with thyme. Grill slices on both sides until browned. Spread bases with sauce, top with eggplant, olive paste and cheese. Bake as directed; top with extra thyme.

PROSCIUTTO AND SAGE

8 slices (120g) prosciutto
2/3 cup (160ml) bottled tomato
    pasta sauce
3/4 cup sun-dried tomatoes in oil,
    drained, chopped
3 teaspoons chopped fresh sage
1/2 cup (50g) grated mozzarella cheese
chopped fresh sage, extra

Cut prosciutto in half lengthways, then in half again; roll up strips. Spread bases with sauce, top with prosciutto, tomatoes and sage; sprinkle with cheese. Bake as directed; top with extra sage.

POTATO AND ROSEMARY

1 large (300g) potato,
    coarsely grated
1 tablespoon olive oil
2 cloves garlic, crushed
1 teaspoon chopped fresh rosemary
2 teaspoons chopped fresh parsley
2/3 cup (160ml) bottled tomato
    pasta sauce
1/4 cup (20g) grated parmesan cheese
fresh rosemary, extra

Squeeze excess moisture from potato. Heat oil in pan, add potato and garlic, cook, stirring, about 5 minutes or until potato is soft and lightly browned; stir in rosemary and parsley. Spread bases with sauce, top with potato mixture; sprinkle with cheese. Bake as directed; top with extra rosemary.

SESAME VEAL TURNOVERS

2 teaspoons olive oil
**½ small (75g) red pepper,
   finely chopped**
**½ small (50g) red Spanish onion,
   finely chopped**
1 clove garlic, crushed
**2 slices (30g) prosciutto,
   finely chopped**
125g minced veal
1 small (60g) egg tomato, chopped
1 tablespoon chopped fresh chives
2 teaspoons ground cumin
¼ cup (60g) mascarpone cheese
6 sheets ready-rolled puff pastry
1 egg, lightly beaten
2 tablespoons sesame seeds

Heat oil in pan, add pepper, onion, garlic and prosciutto, cook, stirring, until onion is soft. Add veal, cook, stirring, until browned. Stir in tomato, chives and cumin; cook, stirring, 2 minutes. Remove from heat, stir in cheese; cool.

Cut 9 x 7cm fluted rounds from each pastry sheet. Spoon 1 teaspoon veal mixture into centre of each round, brush pastry edge with egg, fold over to enclose filling; press edges firmly together to seal. Place turnovers about 3cm apart on lightly greased oven trays, brush with egg; sprinkle with seeds. Bake in moderately hot oven about 20 minutes or until browned.
Makes 54.

- Recipe can be prepared
  a day ahead.
- Storage: Covered, in refrigerator.
- Freeze: Uncooked turnovers suitable.
- Microwave: Not suitable.
- Reheat: Place turnovers on oven
  trays in hot oven 5 minutes.

DOUBLE CHEESE SPIRALS

2 teaspoons olive oil
2 cloves garlic, crushed
1 small (80g) onion, chopped
**¾ cup (60g) finely grated
   parmesan cheese**
¾ cup (150g) feta cheese
**2 teaspoons chopped
   fresh rosemary**
1 tablespoon chopped fresh basil
2 teaspoons tomato paste
5 sheets fillo pastry
¼ cup (60ml) olive oil, extra

Heat oil in pan, add garlic and onion, cook, stirring, until onion is soft; cool 5 minutes. Blend or process onion mixture with cheeses, herbs and paste until smooth. Layer pastry sheets together, brushing each with some of the extra oil. Spread cheese mixture over layered pastry sheets to cover two-thirds of sheet lengthways. Roll up pastry tightly from long cheese-covered side, cover with plastic wrap, refrigerate 1 hour. Cut roll into 1cm slices, place about 3cm apart on greased oven trays, brush with a little more extra oil. Bake in moderate oven about 12 minutes or until browned.
Makes about 25.

- Recipe can be prepared
  a day ahead.
- Storage: Covered, in refrigerator.
- Freeze: Not suitable.
- Microwave: Not suitable.
- Reheat: Place spirals on oven trays
  in hot oven about 5 minutes.

ABOVE: Sesame Veal Turnovers.
ABOVE RIGHT: Tandoori Chicken Nibbles.
RIGHT: Double Cheese Spirals.

Above: China from Elvy Agencies. Above right: Plates from Accoutrement. Right: Platter from Elvy Agencies.

TANDOORI CHICKEN NIBBLES

7 (750g) chicken thigh fillets
½ cup (125ml) plain yogurt
½ cup (125ml) tandoori paste
2 green shallots

CARDAMOM YOGURT SAUCE
½ cup (125ml) plain yogurt
¼ teaspoon ground cardamom

Cut chicken fillets into 6 pieces. Combine chicken, yogurt and paste in bowl; cover, refrigerate 3 hours or overnight. Remove green section from shallots, cut into 2cm lengths, make fine cuts close together, halfway down each 2cm length. Finely chop white section of shallots; reserve for sauce.

Just before serving, cook undrained chicken pieces in batches on heated greased griddle pan or grill until browned all over and tender. Serve chicken pieces on toothpicks with shallot frills. Serve with cardamom yogurt sauce.
Cardamom Yogurt Sauce: Combine reserved shallots with all ingredients in small bowl.
Makes 42.

■ Recipe best made just
  before serving.
■ Freeze: Marinated mixture suitable.
■ Microwave: Not suitable.

THAI CHICKEN PATTIES WITH SWEET CHILLI SAUCE

5 (500g) chicken thigh
   fillets, chopped
1 medium (200g) red pepper, chopped
4 cloves garlic, chopped
½ cup firmly packed
   coriander leaves
2 small fresh red chillies,
   seeded, chopped
1 tablespoon fish sauce
1 egg, lightly beaten
1½ cups (105g) stale breadcrumbs
2 teaspoons finely grated lime rind
3 green shallots, finely chopped
vegetable oil for deep-frying

SWEET CHILLI SAUCE
½ cup (125ml) mild sweet chilli sauce
¼ cup (60ml) lime juice
1 clove garlic, crushed
1 tablespoon fish sauce
2 small fresh red chillies, chopped

Process chicken, pepper, garlic, coriander, chillies, sauce, egg, breadcrumbs and rind until combined. Combine chicken mixture with shallots in bowl. Using floured hands, shape tablespoons of chicken mixture into patties. Just before serving, deep-fry patties in hot oil in batches until browned and cooked; drain. Serve with sweet chilli sauce.

Sweet Chilli Sauce: Combine all ingredients in small bowl, mix well.
Makes about 35.

■ Chicken patties can be prepared a day ahead. Sweet chilli sauce can be made 3 days ahead.
■ Storage: Covered, separately, in refrigerator.
■ Freeze: Not suitable.
■ Microwave: Not suitable.

HONEY-GLAZED CHICKEN WINGS

30 (2.5kg) chicken wings
2 cloves garlic, crushed
3/4 cup (195g) smooth peanut butter
1/2 cup (125ml) water
2 tablespoons soy sauce
2 tablespoons chopped fresh
**   coriander leaves**
1 tablespoon Worcestershire sauce
1 tablespoon honey
2 teaspoons cumin seeds
1 teaspoon sambal oelek

Remove and discard wing tips; separate first and second joints of chicken wings. Whisk remaining ingredients together in large bowl, mix in chicken, cover; refrigerate 3 hours or overnight.

Just before serving, place chicken on wire rack over baking dish. Bake, uncovered, in moderately hot oven about 35 minutes or until chicken is tender. Makes 60.

■ Recipe can be prepared a day ahead.
■ Storage: Covered, in refrigerator.
■ Freeze: Marinated wings suitable.
■ Microwave: Not suitable.

CRAB ROLLS WITH CHILLI PLUM SAUCE

Substitute 300g canned crab for cooked crab in this recipe if you wish.

20g Chinese dried mushrooms
2 teaspoons peanut oil
1 teaspoon grated fresh ginger
2 cloves garlic, crushed
4 green shallots, chopped
1/2 small (75g) red pepper,
**   finely chopped**
300g cooked crab meat,
**   drained, chopped**
1/4 cup drained water chestnuts,
**   chopped**
1 teaspoon sugar
40 small spring-roll wrappers
2 teaspoons cornflour
2 tablespoons water
vegetable oil for deep-frying

CHILLI PLUM SAUCE
2 teaspoons peanut oil
1 clove garlic, crushed
1 teaspoon grated fresh ginger
1/3 cup (80ml) plum sauce
1/3 cup (80ml) mild sweet chilli sauce
1 tablespoon brown sugar
2/3 cup (160ml) chicken stock

Place mushrooms in heatproof bowl, cover with boiling water, stand 20 minutes, drain. Remove and discard stems, finely chop caps.

Heat oil in pan, add ginger, garlic, shallots and pepper, cook, stirring, until peppers are soft; cool 5 minutes. Stir in mushrooms, crab, chestnuts and sugar.

Place 1 tablespoon crab mixture across a corner of 1 wrapper, brush edges with a little blended cornflour and water, fold in sides, roll up to enclose filling. Repeat with remaining crab mixture, wrappers and cornflour mixture.

Just before serving, deep-fry crab rolls in hot oil in batches until browned; drain. Serve with chilli plum sauce.

Chilli Plum Sauce: Heat oil in pan, add garlic and ginger, cook, stirring, until fragrant. Add remaining ingredients, simmer, uncovered, about 10 minutes or until reduced to about 1 cup (250ml). Makes 40.

■ Rolls can be assembled a day ahead. Sauce can be made 3 days ahead.
■ Storage: Covered, separately, in refrigerator.
■ Freeze: Uncooked rolls and sauce suitable.
■ Microwave: Crab mixture and sauce suitable.

Clockwise from back: Honey-Glazed Chicken Wings; Thai Chicken Patties with Sweet Chilli Sauce; Crab Rolls with Chilli Plum Sauce.

China, serviettes and serviette rings from Accoutrement; glasses from Art House.

LAMB KOFTA WITH HUMMUS DIP

500g minced lamb
200g sausage mince
1 medium (150g) onion, finely grated
1 egg, lightly beaten
2 tablespoons chopped fresh coriander leaves
1 teaspoon ground cinnamon
1 teaspoon ground cumin
1 tablespoon tomato paste
1/2 cup (35g) stale breadcrumbs
vegetable oil for deep-frying

HUMMUS DIP
2 x 310g cans chickpeas, rinsed, drained
1 clove garlic, crushed
1/4 cup (60ml) tahini
1/4 cup (60ml) lemon juice
1/2 cup (125ml) buttermilk
1/4 cup (60ml) water

Combine lamb and sausage mince, onion, egg, coriander, spices, paste and breadcrumbs in bowl; shape table-spoons of mixture into ovals, place on tray, cover; refrigerate 30 minutes.

Just before serving, deep-fry kofta in hot oil in batches until browned and cooked through; drain on absorbent paper. Serve with hummus dip.

Hummus Dip: Blend or process all ingredients until smooth.
Makes about 40.

■ Kofta can be prepared a day ahead. Hummus can be made a day ahead.
■ Storage: Covered, separately, in refrigerator.
■ Freeze: Uncooked kofta suitable.
■ Microwave: Not suitable.

DEEP-FRIED SPICY OLIVES

300g large (about 50) black olives, seeded
3 cloves garlic, crushed
1 teaspoon sambal oelek
plain flour
3 eggs, lightly beaten
1 2/3 cups (120g) stale breadcrumbs
2/3 cup (50g) finely grated parmesan cheese
2 tablespoons chopped fresh basil
2 tablespoons chopped fresh parsley
2 teaspoons chopped fresh thyme
vegetable oil for deep-frying

Combine olives, garlic and sambal oelek in bowl, cover, refrigerate several hours or overnight.

Toss olives in flour, shake away excess flour. Dip olives in eggs, then in combined breadcrumbs, cheese and herbs. Repeat coating process, using eggs and breadcrumb mixture, place on tray, cover; refrigerate 1 hour.

Just before serving, deep-fry olives in hot oil in batches until browned; drain on absorbent paper.
Makes about 50.

- Olives can be prepared 1 day ahead.
- Storage: Covered, in refrigerator.
- Freeze: Not suitable.
- Microwave: Not suitable.

SPICY CHICKPEA FRITTERS

1 cup (150g) chickpea flour
1 cup (150g) self-raising flour
1 teaspoon garam masala
1 teaspoon ground turmeric
2 teaspoons mild curry powder
1 tablespoon chopped fresh
    coriander leaves
2 medium (240g) carrots,
    finely grated
2 medium (240g) zucchini,
    finely grated
3 green shallots, finely chopped
1 cup (250ml) water, approximately
vegetable oil for deep-frying

TAHINI SAUCE
1/4 cup (60ml) tahini
2 tablespoons lemon juice
pinch cayenne pepper
1/2 cup (125ml) sour cream
1/4 cup (60ml) water
1 teaspoon ground cumin

Sift flours into bowl, stir in spices, coriander, grated vegetables and shallots. Stir in enough water to give a sticky mixture.

Just before serving, drop tablespoons of mixture in hot oil in batches; cook until browned and cooked through. Drain on absorbent paper; serve with tahini sauce.
Tahini Sauce: Combine all ingredients in bowl; mix well.
Makes about 40.

- Fritters best made just before serving. Tahini sauce can be made 1 day ahead.
- Storage: Covered, in refrigerator.
- Freeze: Not suitable.
- Microwave: Not suitable.

RED PEPPER TARTLETS

3 medium (600g) red peppers
1 tablespoon olive oil
1 small (100g) red Spanish onion,
    finely chopped
2 tablespoons pine nuts, toasted
1/4 cup (40g) finely chopped seedless
    black olives
1/4 cup sun-dried tomatoes in oil,
    drained, chopped
2 tablespoons chopped fresh basil
4 x 50g packets of 12 savoury
    tartlet cases
2 tablespoons finely grated
    parmesan cheese

Quarter peppers, remove seeds and membranes. Grill peppers, skin side up, until skin blisters and blackens. Peel away skin, finely chop peppers. Heat oil in pan, add onion, nuts, olives and tomatoes, cook, stirring, until onion is soft. Add peppers and basil, cook 2 minutes.

Just before serving, place pastry cases on oven trays, divide pepper mixture among cases; sprinkle with cheese. Bake in hot oven about 5 minutes or until heated through.
Makes 48.

- Pepper mixture can be made a day ahead.
- Storage: Covered, in refrigerator.
- Freeze: Not suitable.
- Microwave: Not suitable.

LEFT: Clockwise from back left: Lamb Kofta with Hummus Dip; Deep-Fried Spicy Olives; Spicy Chickpea Fritters.
BELOW: Red Pepper Tartlets.

Left: Plates and server from Dinosaur Designs.

Quiches

Individual quiches are always popular, and ours made with these fabulous fillings will disappear from the serving platter in seconds. The pastry cases can be made 2 days ahead and kept in an airtight container; quiches can be baked up to 2 hours before serving. Only unfilled pastry cases are suitable to freeze; none of these recipes is suitable to microwave. The basic pastry recipe makes 36 cases, and each filling recipe makes enough for 36 quiches. Reheat on oven trays in hot oven about 15 minutes.

BASIC PASTRY

1½ cups (225g) plain flour
125g cold butter, chopped
1 egg, lightly beaten
2 teaspoons freshly ground black pepper
1 teaspoon lemon juice, approximately

Grease 3 x 12 hole deep patty pan trays (2 tablespoon capacity).

Sift flour into bowl, rub in butter (or process together). Add egg, pepper and enough juice to make ingredients just cling together (or process until ingredients just come together). Press dough into a ball, knead gently on floured surface until smooth. Wrap in plastic; refrigerate 30 minutes.

Divide pastry in half. Roll each half between sheets of baking paper until 2mm thick. Cut 18 x 6.5cm fluted rounds from each half of pastry; re-roll pastry scraps. Press rounds into prepared pans, prick well with skewer or fork. Cover; refrigerate 30 minutes.

Bake in moderately hot oven about 10 minutes or until lightly browned; cool. Fill pastry cases with preferred quiche mixture. Bake in moderate oven about 15 minutes or until set; remove quiches from trays.

BASIC QUICHE MIXTURE

½ cup (125ml) milk
½ cup (125ml) cream
2 eggs, lightly beaten

Whisk all ingredients together in a bowl.

PROSCIUTTO AND BRIE

2 teaspoons olive oil
1 small (80g) onion, finely chopped
4 slices (60g) prosciutto, chopped
2 teaspoons chopped fresh rosemary
125g brie, sliced
1 quantity basic quiche mixture
fresh rosemary leaves, extra

Heat oil in pan, add onion and prosciutto, cook, stirring, until onion is soft; stir in rosemary. Divide brie and prosciutto mixture among pastry cases, top with basic quiche mixture. Bake as directed; top with extra rosemary.

PUMPKIN AND HERB

1 cup cold cooked mashed pumpkin
1 teaspoon chopped fresh basil
2 teaspoons chopped fresh parsley
½ teaspoon chopped fresh thyme
½ teaspoon chopped fresh rosemary
1 quantity basic quiche mixture
fresh coriander leaves

Combine pumpkin, herbs and basic quiche mixture in bowl; divide among pastry cases. Bake as directed; top with coriander leaves.

LORRAINE

2 teaspoons olive oil
1 medium (150g) onion, finely chopped
3 bacon rashers, finely chopped
1/4 teaspoon ground nutmeg
½ cup (60g) grated gruyere cheese
1 quantity basic quiche mixture

Heat oil in pan, add onion and bacon, cook, stirring, until onion is soft, transfer to bowl; cool. Stir in nutmeg and half the cheese, combine with basic quiche mixture; divide among pastry cases, sprinkle with remaining cheese; bake as directed.

SMOKED SALMON

1 teaspoon olive oil
4 green shallots, finely chopped
200g sliced smoked salmon, chopped
1 quantity basic quiche mixture
green shallot strips, extra

Heat oil in pan, add shallots, cook, stirring, until soft, transfer to bowl, add salmon; cool. Stir in basic quiche mixture; divide among pastry cases. Bake as directed; top with extra shallot.

EGGPLANT, PEPPER AND SUN-DRIED TOMATO

2 (120g) finger eggplants
1 tablespoon olive oil
1 small (150g) red pepper
2 tablespoons sun-dried tomatoes in oil, drained, chopped
1/3 cup (25g) finely grated parmesan cheese
1 tablespoon chopped fresh basil
1 quantity basic quiche mixture
red pepper strips, extra
fresh basil leaves, extra

Slice eggplants thinly lengthways, brush both sides with oil. Place on oven tray, bake in moderate oven about 15 minutes or until tender; cool. Chop eggplant finely. Quarter pepper, remove seeds and membranes. Grill pepper, skin side

CHICKEN AND LEEK

2 teaspoons olive oil
1 clove garlic, crushed
½ small (100g) leek, finely sliced
½ cup (100g) finely chopped
    cooked chicken
1 quantity basic quiche mixture
thin strips lemon rind
fresh basil leaves

Heat oil in pan, add garlic and leek, cook, stirring, until leek is soft, transfer to bowl, add chicken; cool. Stir in basic quiche mixture; divide among pastry cases. Bake as directed; top with lemon rind and basil.

MUSHROOM AND SHALLOTS

2 teaspoons olive oil
4 green shallots, chopped
150g mushrooms, finely chopped
2 teaspoons chopped fresh
    coriander leaves
1 quantity basic quiche mixture

Heat oil in pan, add shallots and mushrooms, cook, stirring, until mushrooms are soft, transfer to bowl; cool. Stir in coriander and basic quiche mixture; divide among pastry cases. Bake as directed.

CRAB AND DILL

2 teaspoons olive oil
6 green shallots, finely chopped
2 x 170g cans crab meat, drained
1 tablespoon grated lemon rind
1 tablespoon chopped fresh dill
1 quantity basic quiche mixture
tiny lemon wedges
fresh dill sprigs, extra

Heat oil in pan, add shallots, cook, stirring, until shallots are soft, transfer to bowl. Stir in crab meat, rind, dill, then basic quiche mixture; divide among pastry cases. Bake as directed; top with lemon wedges and extra dill.

up, until skin blisters and blackens. Peel away skin, finely chop pepper. Combine eggplant, pepper, tomatoes, cheese, basil and basic quiche mixture in bowl; divide among pastry cases. Bake as directed; top with extra pepper and extra basil.

RED SALMON

210g can red salmon, drained, flaked
3 green shallots, finely chopped
2 teaspoons chopped fresh thyme
1 tablespoon seeded mustard
1 tablespoon drained capers,
    chopped
1 quantity basic quiche mixture

Combine all ingredients in bowl; divide among pastry cases. Bake as directed; top with extra thyme, if desired.

SPINACH AND RICOTTA

2 teaspoons olive oil
1 small (80g) onion, finely chopped
2 medium (160g) silverbeet leaves,
    finely chopped
¾ cup (150g) ricotta cheese
pinch cayenne pepper
½ cup (40g) finely grated
    parmesan cheese
1 quantity basic quiche mixture
¼ cup (40g) pine nuts, toasted

Heat oil in pan, add onion, cook, stirring, until onion is soft, add silverbeet, cover; cool. Transfer to bowl, stir in ricotta, pepper, parmesan and basic quiche mixture; divide among pastry cases; sprinkle with nuts. Bake as directed.

1. Prosciutto and Brie 2. Lorraine 3. Chicken and Leek 4. Red Salmon 5. Eggplant, Pepper and Sun-Dried Tomato 6. Spinach and Ricotta 7. Mushroom and Shallots 8. Smoked Salmon 9. Pumpkin and Herb 10. Crab and Dill.

BACON, PINE NUT AND HERB-FILLED MUSHROOMS

2 teaspoons olive oil
1 tablespoon pine nuts
3 cloves garlic, crushed
2 green shallots, finely chopped
2 bacon rashers, finely chopped
2 tablespoons chopped fresh parsley
30 (500g) button mushrooms
plain flour
2 eggs, lightly beaten
2 teaspoons milk
3/4 cup (75g) packaged breadcrumbs
vegetable oil for deep-frying

Heat olive oil in pan, add nuts, stir until lightly browned. Add garlic, shallots, bacon and parsley, cook, stirring, until bacon is crisp. Remove stems from mushrooms, fill caps with mixture, pressing down firmly.

Just before serving, toss mushrooms gently in flour, shake away excess, dip in combined eggs and milk, then breadcrumbs. Deep-fry mushrooms in batches in hot oil until browned; drain. Makes 30.

■ Uncooked mushrooms can be filled a day ahead.
■ Storage: Covered, in refrigerator.
■ Freeze: Not suitable.
■ Microwave: Not suitable.

SPINACH CHEESE PUFFS

2 teaspoons olive oil
1 large (200g) onion, finely chopped
2 cloves garlic, crushed
2 teaspoons sweet paprika
1 bunch (500g) English spinach, chopped
3/4 cup (110g) self-raising flour
3/4 cup (60g) grated parmesan cheese
3 eggs, lightly beaten
vegetable oil for deep-frying

Heat olive oil in pan, add onion, garlic and paprika, cook, stirring, until onion is soft; cool. Boil, steam or microwave spinach until just tender, drain, squeeze with hands to remove moisture; chop spinach finely. Combine onion mixture, spinach, flour, cheese and eggs in bowl; mix well.

Just before serving, drop tablespoons of mixture into hot oil in batches, deep-fry until browned and cooked through; drain on absorbent paper.
Makes about 30.

■ Recipe best made just before serving.
■ Freeze: Not suitable.
■ Microwave: Not suitable.

LEFT: From back: Spinach Cheese Puffs; Bacon, Pine Nut and Herb-Filled Mushrooms. RIGHT: Chunky Cajun Potato Wedges.

Right: China from Villeroy & Boch; trivets, cloth and serviette rings from Morris Home & Garden Wares.

CHUNKY CAJUN POTATO WEDGES

8 medium (1.6kg) old potatoes
1/4 cup (60ml) olive oil
90g butter, melted
2 tablespoons ground cumin
2 tablespoons Cajun seasoning

PESTO DIPPING SAUCE
300ml sour cream
1/4 cup (60ml) bottled pesto
1/4 cup (20g) finely grated parmesan cheese

SWEET CHILLI DIPPING SAUCE
1/3 cup (80ml) mild sweet chilli sauce
300ml sour cream

Cut unpeeled potatoes in half, cut each half into 4 wedges. Boil, steam or microwave potatoes until just tender; cool. Combine oil, butter and spices in large bowl, add potato wedges in batches, coat evenly with spice mixture.

Place wedges on oven trays, bake, uncovered, in hot oven about 45 minutes or until crisp. Serve with dipping sauces.
Pesto Dipping Sauce: Combine all ingredients in bowl, mix well.
Sweet Chilli Dipping Sauce: Combine all ingredients in bowl, mix well.
Makes 64 wedges.

■ Wedges best baked just before serving. Dipping sauces can be made a day ahead.
■ Storage: Sauces, covered, separately, in refrigerator.
■ Freeze: Not suitable.
■ Microwave: Not suitable.

MUSSELS WITH ROASTED GARLIC MAYONNAISE

1 small (150g) red pepper
30 small (about 500g) mussels
1 small (80g) onion, finely chopped
1 cup (250ml) dry white wine
1 bay leaf
1 large (100g) silverbeet leaf,
finely shredded

ROASTED GARLIC MAYONNAISE
1 bulb (90g) garlic
1 tablespoon light olive oil
1 egg yolk
1 teaspoon Dijon mustard
1 tablespoon lemon juice
2/3 cup (160ml) light olive oil, extra
pinch cayenne pepper
1 teaspoon freshly ground
black pepper
1 teaspoon chopped fresh thyme

Quarter pepper, remove seeds and membranes. Grill pepper, skin side up, until skin blisters and blackens; peel away skin. Cut pepper into thin strips.

Scrub mussels, remove beards. Combine onion, wine, bay leaf and mussels in pan, cook, covered, over high heat about 5 minutes or until shells open. Drain, discard liquid and any unopened mussels. Remove and discard half of each mussel shell, remove mussels from remaining shells.

Place mussel shells on oven trays; divide silverbeet and pepper equally among them, top each with 1 mussel and some mayonnaise.

Just before serving, grill mussels until heated through.

Roasted Garlic Mayonnaise: Place whole garlic bulb on oven tray, drizzle with oil. Bake, uncovered, in moderately hot oven about 45 minutes or until very soft. Stand garlic 15 minutes, cut in half horizontally, squeeze out garlic pulp. Blend or process garlic pulp, egg yolk, mustard and juice until smooth. Add extra oil in a thin stream while motor is operating. Stir in peppers and thyme.

Makes 30.

■ Recipe can be prepared a day ahead.
■ Storage: Mussels and mayonnaise, covered, separately in refrigerator.
■ Freeze: Not suitable.
■ Microwave: Not suitable.

POTATO ONION TURNOVERS

1 small (120g) potato, finely chopped
1 teaspoon vegetable oil
60g (about 1/2 stick) cabanossi,
finely chopped
1 small (80g) onion, finely chopped
1 tablespoon chopped fresh
coriander leaves
1/3 cup (50g) chopped unsalted
roasted peanuts
1 tablespoon mild sweet chilli sauce
5 sheets ready-rolled puff pastry
1 egg, lightly beaten

NUTTY BEEF ROLLS

2 teaspoons olive oil
5 green shallots, finely chopped
1 teaspoon ground cumin
1 teaspoon chopped fresh rosemary
2 bacon rashers, finely chopped
2 bottled jalapeno peppers, drained,
    finely chopped
1/3 cup (50g) finely chopped
    pistachio nuts
450g piece beef eye-fillet
2 tablespoons honey
1 teaspoon Dijon mustard
1 tablespoon soy sauce
2 tablespoons chopped pistachio
    nuts, extra

Heat oil in pan, add shallots, cumin, rosemary, bacon and peppers, cook, stirring, until bacon is crisp; stir in nuts. Cut beef into 3mm slices, shape each slice into an 8cm square with hand or blade of knife. Place rounded teaspoons shallot mixture on each slice of beef, roll up to enclose filling. Place rolls on greased oven tray. Combine honey, mustard and sauce in small pan, stir over heat until warm. Brush rolls with honey mixture; sprinkle with extra nuts.

Just before serving, bake in moderate oven about 10 minutes or until beef is just tender.
Makes about 25.

■ Rolls can be prepared a day ahead.
■ Storage: Covered, in refrigerator.
■ Freeze: Uncooked unglazed
   rolls suitable.
■ Microwave: Not suitable.

LEFT: Mussels with Roasted Garlic Mayonnaise.
BELOW: From back: Potato Onion Turnovers; Nutty Beef Rolls.

Left: China from Villeroy & Boch; silver containers and beads from Morris Home & Garden Wares.
Below: China and cloth from The Bay Tree Kitchen Shop.

Boil, steam or microwave potato until just tender; drain. Heat oil in pan, add cabanossi, cook, stirring, until browned; drain. Add onion to same pan, cook, stirring, until onion is soft; drain. Combine potato in bowl with cabanossi, onion, coriander, half the peanuts and sauce.

Cut 9 x 6.5cm rounds from each sheet of pastry. Place 1 teaspoon of potato mixture in centre of pastry rounds, brush edges with water, fold over to enclose filling, press edges together with fork to seal. Place turnovers about 3cm apart on greased oven trays, brush with egg; sprinkle with remaining peanuts. Bake in moderate oven about 20 minutes or until browned. Makes 45.

■ Recipe can be made a day ahead.
■ Storage: Covered, in refrigerator.
■ Freeze: Uncooked turnovers suitable.
■ Microwave: Potato suitable.
■ Reheat: Place turnovers on oven
   trays in hot oven for 5 minutes.

KUMARA BACON CONES

You need 30 pastry cones for this recipe; they are made using 5cm x 15cm cream cone tins. Bake the cones in batches.

1 sheet ready-rolled puff pastry
1 egg yolk

FILLING
1 small (250g) kumara
30g butter
1 teaspoon grated fresh ginger
1 small (80g) onion, finely chopped
1 bacon rasher, finely chopped
2 teaspoons chopped fresh rosemary
1/4 cup (60ml) sour cream
2 tablespoons finely grated parmesan cheese

Lightly grease the cream cone tins. Cut pastry sheet into 1.5cm strips, cut each strip in half crossways. Moisten 1 edge of strip with water. Starting at point of 1 tin, wind 1 strip around each tin, overlapping the moistened edge; do not stretch pastry. Repeat with remaining tins. Place tins about 3cm apart on lightly greased oven trays, brush lightly with egg yolk. Bake in moderately hot oven about 10 minutes or until browned. Slip tins from pastry cones. Repeat process until you have 30 cones.

Spoon filling into piping bag fitted with small star tube. Pipe filling into cones, place on oven trays.

Just before serving, bake in moderately hot oven about 5 minutes or until heated through.

Filling: Boil, steam or microwave kumara until soft; drain, cool. Melt butter in pan, add ginger, onion and bacon, cook, stirring, until onion is soft, cool. Blend or process kumara, onion mixture, rosemary, cream and cheese until smooth.

Makes 30.

■ Cones and filling can be made a day ahead.
■ Storage: Cones, in airtight container. Filling, covered, in refrigerator.
■ Freeze: Unfilled cones suitable.
■ Microwave: Kumara suitable.

SPICY TIKKA PRAWNS WITH SPINACH RAITA

30 (1kg) large uncooked prawns
1/4 cup (60ml) tikka paste
1/2 cup (125ml) plain yogurt
1/4 cup (60ml) lemon juice
2 tablespoons chopped fresh coriander leaves

SPINACH RAITA
1/2 bunch (250g) English spinach, chopped
1 cup (250ml) plain yogurt
1 small clove garlic, crushed
1 teaspoon ground cumin
1 tablespoon lemon juice

Shell and devein prawns, leaving tails intact. Combine prawns, paste, yogurt, juice and coriander in bowl, cover; refrigerate 3 hours or overnight.

Just before serving, grill drained prawns until just tender. Serve with spinach raita.

Spinach Raita: Boil, microwave or steam spinach until just wilted, drain, cool. Blend or process spinach with remaining ingredients.

Makes 30.

■ Recipe best made just before serving. Prawns best marinated a day ahead.
■ Storage: Covered, separately, in refrigerator.
■ Freeze: Not suitable.
■ Microwave: Spinach suitable.

RIGHT: Spicy Tikka Prawns with Spinach Raita.
BELOW: Kumara Bacon Cones.

Below: Plate, tray and cloth from Accoutrement.

SEAFOOD TOAST TRIANGLES

1kg uncooked prawns
2 cloves garlic, crushed
2 tablespoons chopped fresh
    coriander leaves
2 tablespoons mild sweet
    chilli sauce
1 tablespoon honey
3 teaspoons mango chutney
8 slices frozen white bread
60g butter, melted
70g mozzarella cheese,
    finely chopped
3 teaspoons sesame seeds

Shell and devein prawns, chop finely. Combine prawns, garlic, coriander, sauce, honey and chutney in bowl. Cut crusts from bread, cut each slice into 4 triangles, brush both sides with butter. Place triangles on oven trays, top with cheese, then prawn mixture; sprinkle with seeds. Bake in moderately hot oven about 15 minutes or until browned. Makes 32.

■ Recipe can be prepared
    3 hours ahead.
■ Storage: Covered, in refrigerator.
■ Freeze: Uncooked seafood toast
    triangles suitable.
■ Microwave: Not suitable.
■ Reheat: Place triangles on oven trays
    in hot oven for about 5 minutes.

FRIED MOZZARELLA

500g piece mozzarella cheese
plain flour
5 eggs, lightly beaten
1 clove garlic, crushed
1½ cups (300g) couscous
1 cup (100g) packaged breadcrumbs
½ cup (40g) grated parmesan cheese
½ cup finely chopped fresh basil
vegetable oil for deep-frying

SPICY TOMATO SAUCE
1 small (150g) red pepper
425g can tomatoes
1 clove garlic, crushed
½ cup (125ml) bottled tomato
    pasta sauce
2 small (260g) green cucumbers,
    peeled, seeded, chopped
1 teaspoon sugar
1 small fresh red chilli,
    finely chopped

Cut mozzarella into 2cm pieces, toss in flour, shake away excess flour. Dip into combined eggs and garlic, then combined couscous, breadcrumbs, parmesan and basil; press on firmly. Repeat coating process; place on tray, refrigerate 30 minutes.

Just before serving, deep-fry mozzarella in hot oil in batches until browned; drain on absorbent paper. Serve with spicy tomato sauce.
Spicy Tomato Sauce: Quarter pepper, remove seeds and membranes. Grill

pepper, skin side up, until skin blisters and blackens. Peel away skin, roughly chop pepper. Blend or process pepper with remaining ingredients until smooth. Place in pan, simmer, uncovered, about 10 minutes or until slightly thickened. Makes about 50.

■ Mozzarella can be coated 2 days
    ahead. Sauce can be made
    2 days ahead.
■ Storage: Covered, separately,
    in refrigerator.
■ Freeze: Not suitable.
■ Microwave: Not suitable.

SHEPHERD'S POTATO PIES

35 baby (1.4kg) new potatoes
2 teaspoons vegetable oil
1 small (80g) onion, finely chopped
250g minced lamb
1 medium (130g) tomato, peeled,
    finely chopped
¼ cup (60ml) tomato sauce
2 teaspoons Worcestershire sauce
1 teaspoon chopped fresh rosemary
20g soft butter
1 tablespoon grated parmesan cheese
3 teaspoons chopped fresh parsley

Boil, steam or microwave potatoes until tender; cool. Cut tops from potatoes; discard tops. Using a melon baller, scoop a small hollow into each potato; reserve scooped-out pieces of potato.

Place potatoes on oven tray. Heat oil in pan, add onion, cook, stirring, until onion is soft. Add lamb, cook, stirring, until browned. Stir in tomato, sauces and rosemary, cook, stirring, few minutes or until slightly thickened; cool 5 minutes. Spoon lamb mixture into piping bag fitted with plain tube; pipe lamb mixture into potatoes.

Blend or process reserved potato pieces with butter, cheese and parsley until just smooth (do not over-process). Spoon potato mixture into piping bag fitted with fluted tube. Pipe potato mixture over lamb mixture. Bake in moderately hot oven about 15 minutes or until heated through.
Makes 35.

■ Recipe can be prepared
    2 days ahead.
■ Storage: Covered, in refrigerator.
■ Freeze: Not suitable.
■ Microwave: Potatoes suitable.
■ Reheat: Place potato pies on oven
    trays in hot oven for about 5 minutes.

LEFT: From back: Seafood Toast Triangles; Fried Mozzarella.
BELOW: Shepherd's Potato Pies.

Left: China and wire stand from Corso De' Fiori; serviette rings from Opus Design; glasses from Pacific East India Co. Below: China from Villeroy & Boch; wooden spoons from Morris Home & Garden Wares.

Heavenly Half-Shells

*Oysters and mussels make great finger food, coming as they do in a self-presentation pack!
Uncooked oyster recipes can be made several hours ahead and stored, covered, in refrigerator. Grilled oyster
and all mussel recipes are best made just before serving. None of the following recipes is suitable to freeze or
microwave. Each topping is enough for 12 oysters or mussels in their half-shells.*

Mussels

*Scrub 12 fresh mussels, remove beards.
Heat 2 cups (500ml) water in pan;
add mussels, cook, covered, over high
heat about 5 minutes or until shells
open. Drain; discard liquid and any
unopened mussels. Discard top half of
each mussel shell.*

HOT AND CREAMY SALSA

1 green shallot, finely chopped
2 teaspoons chopped fresh
   coriander leaves
1 tablespoon finely chopped
   red pepper
2 teaspoons sour cream
1 tablespoon balsamic vinegar
1/4 teaspoon ground cumin
1/4 teaspoon chilli powder

Combine all ingredients in small bowl;
spoon over mussels.

GREEN PEPPERCORN AND BRANDY

2 teaspoons drained green
   peppercorns
2 teaspoons brandy
1/3 cup (80ml) cream
1 teaspoon French mustard

Combine peppercorns, brandy, cream
and mustard in small pan; simmer,
uncovered, about 5 minutes or until
sauce thickens slightly. Spoon over
mussels; serve warm.

RICH TOMATO AND BASIL

1 teaspoon olive oil
1 small (80g) onion,
    finely chopped
1 clove garlic, crushed
1/3 cup (80ml) bottled tomato
    pasta sauce
1 tablespoon chopped
    fresh basil

Heat oil in pan, add onion and garlic, cook, stirring, until onion is soft, add sauce and basil; simmer, uncovered, about 5 minutes or until sauce thickens. Spoon over mussels; serve warm.

GARLIC PARSLEY BUTTER

20g butter
3 cloves garlic, crushed
2 teaspoons chopped
    fresh parsley
1 1/2 tablespoons olive oil

Melt butter in pan, add garlic, parsley and oil, cook, stirring, few minutes until garlic is soft. Spoon over mussels; serve warm.

MUSHROOM AND BASIL

30g butter
2 green shallots, finely chopped
50g mushrooms, finely chopped
1/4 cup (60ml) dry white wine
1 tablespoon chopped fresh basil

Melt butter in pan, add shallots and mushrooms, cook, stirring, until mushrooms are soft, add wine and basil; simmer, uncovered, 5 minutes. Spoon over mussels; serve warm.

Oysters

Remove 12 fresh oysters from shells. Drain oysters on absorbent paper; wash and dry shells. Return each oyster to 1 half-shell before assembly, discard other half.

KILPATRICK

1 bacon rasher, finely chopped
1 green shallot, finely chopped
1 tablespoon Worcestershire sauce

Add bacon to small heated pan, cook, stirring, until crisp; drain. Combine bacon in bowl with remaining ingredients; spoon over oysters. Grill until heated through.

WASABI AND CHILLI

3/4 teaspoon wasabi powder
1 1/2 tablespoons rice vinegar
2 small fresh red chillies,
    finely chopped

Combine wasabi and vinegar in bowl, spoon over oysters; sprinkle with chillies.

LIME AND CHILLI

1 tablespoon lime juice
1 teaspoon chopped fresh
    coriander leaves
1 clove garlic, crushed
1 teaspoon mild sweet chilli sauce
1 teaspoon peanut oil

Combine all ingredients in small bowl, spoon over oysters.

GINGER AND SOY SAUCE

1 teaspoon grated fresh ginger
3 teaspoons salt-reduced soy sauce
1 teaspoon water
1 green shallot, finely chopped

Combine all ingredients in small bowl; spoon over oysters.

HERB, GARLIC AND BREADCRUMBS

1/3 cup (25g) stale breadcrumbs
30g butter, melted
2 teaspoons chopped fresh parsley
1 clove garlic, crushed
1/4 teaspoon ground cumin

Combine all ingredients in bowl; spoon over oysters. Grill until lightly browned.

OYSTER TOPPINGS
1. Wasabi and Chilli 2. Herb, Garlic and Breadcrumbs 3. Kilpatrick 4. Lime and Chilli 5. Ginger and Soy Sauce.
MUSSEL TOPPINGS
6. Hot and Creamy Salsa 7. Rich Tomato and Basil 8. Green Peppercorn and Brandy 9. Mushroom and Basil 10. Garlic Parsley Butter.

Shell plates from Accoutrement; rectangular and leaf plates from The Bay Tree Kitchen Shop; fish plate, rack, oyster forks and star plate from Orson & Blake Collectables.

SPICY CHICKEN BITES

3 large (600g) chicken breast fillets
1/4 cup (60ml) low-fat sour cream
1 tablespoon Dijon mustard
1/4 cup (60ml) milk
2 tablespoons Cajun seasoning
3 teaspoons ground cumin
1/3 cup (40g) chopped walnuts
2/3 cup (100g) plain flour
vegetable oil for deep-frying

MUSTARD SAUCE
3/4 cup (180ml) low-fat sour cream
1 tablespoon Dijon mustard
2 tablespoons mayonnaise
1 tablespoon chopped fresh parsley

Chop chicken into 2cm pieces, combine in bowl with cream, mustard and milk. Drain chicken, toss in combined spices, nuts and flour; shake off excess spice mixture.

Just before serving, deep-fry chicken in hot oil in batches until browned and cooked; drain. Serve with mustard sauce.
Mustard Sauce: Combine all ingredients in bowl; mix well.
Makes about 60.

- Chicken best made just before serving. Mustard sauce can be made 1 day ahead.
- Storage: Covered, in refrigerator.
- Freeze: Not suitable.
- Microwave: Not suitable.

SPICY MOROCCAN LAMB TRIANGLES

2 tablespoons olive oil
8 (640g) lamb fillets
4 cloves garlic, crushed
2 medium (300g) onions, chopped
3 teaspoons ground cinnamon
3 teaspoons ground cumin
3 teaspoons ground ginger
3/4 cup (120g) finely chopped raisins
1 cup (160g) blanched almonds, toasted, finely chopped
1/4 cup chopped fresh coriander leaves
22 sheets (375g packet) fillo pastry
80g butter, melted

YOGURT CUMIN SAUCE
1 1/2 cups (375ml) plain yogurt
2 tablespoons lemon juice
2 teaspoons ground cumin
1 teaspoon sugar

Heat half the oil in pan, cook lamb in batches until browned all over and tender; cool. Heat remaining oil in same pan, add garlic, onions and spices, cook, stirring, until onions are soft. Chop lamb finely, combine in bowl with onion mixture, raisins, nuts and coriander.

To prevent fillo from drying out, cover with damp tea-towel until ready to use. Layer 2 sheets pastry together, brushing each with a little butter. Cut layered sheets into 4 strips lengthways.

Place 1 tablespoon lamb mixture at 1 end of each strip. Fold a corner end of pastry diagonally across filling to other edge to form a triangle. Continue folding to end of strip, retaining triangular shape. Repeat with remaining pastry, more butter and lamb mixture. Place triangles on greased oven trays, brush with more butter. Bake in moderately hot oven about 15 minutes or until browned. Serve with yogurt cumin sauce.
Yogurt Cumin Sauce: Combine all ingredients in bowl.
Makes 44.

- Lamb mixture and sauce can be made 1 day ahead.
- Storage: Covered, separately, in refrigerator.
- Freeze: Uncooked triangles suitable.
- Microwave: Lamb filling suitable.
- Reheat: Place lamb triangles on oven trays in hot oven for about 5 minutes.

LEFT: Spicy Chicken Bites.
BELOW: Spicy Moroccan Lamb Triangles.

Left: China from Accoutrement; tiles from Fred Pazotti.
Below: China from Kim Elvy Agencies.

FRIED CHEESE TRIANGLES

8 slices white bread
1/2 cup (125ml) sour cream
1 cup (125g) grated gruyere cheese
3 teaspoons Dijon mustard
2 tablespoons chopped fresh chives
1 teaspoon chopped fresh thyme
plain flour
2 eggs, lightly beaten
2 tablespoons milk
3/4 cup (75g) packaged breadcrumbs
1/2 cup (40g) finely grated
   parmesan cheese
vegetable oil for shallow-frying

Spread 4 slices bread with combined cream, gruyere, mustard and herbs, top with remaining slices of bread; press down firmly. Remove crusts from each sandwich, cut into 8 triangles. Toss triangles in flour, shake away excess flour. Dip triangles in combined eggs and milk, then in combined breadcrumbs and parmesan; place on tray, refrigerate 1 hour.

Just before serving, shallow-fry the triangles in hot oil until browned; drain on absorbent paper.
Makes 32.

■ Sandwiches can be made
  a day ahead.
■ Storage: Covered, in refrigerator.
■ Freeze: Uncooked triangles suitable.
■ Microwave: Not suitable.

CRISPY PROSCIUTTO HASH BROWN PATTIES

30g butter
1 green shallot, finely chopped
1 clove garlic, crushed
2 medium (400g) old potatoes,
   coarsely grated
2 teaspoons chopped fresh sage
2 tablespoons olive oil
8 slices (120g) prosciutto
1/3 cup (35g) grated mozzarella cheese

Melt butter in pan, add shallot and garlic, cook, stirring, until shallot is soft. Add potatoes and sage, stir over heat until potatoes are sticky; cool.

Using wet fingers, shape rounded teaspoons of potato mixture into patties; flatten slightly. Heat half the oil in a large pan, add half the patties, cook a few minutes each side until crisp. Repeat with remaining oil and patties.

Quarter prosciutto slices, roll up from short sides, place on top of patties, sprinkle with cheese.

Just before serving, bake in moderate oven about 10 minutes or until cheese is melted.
Makes about 32.

■ Hash browns can be prepared
  3 hours ahead.
■ Storage: Covered, in refrigerator.
■ Freeze: Not suitable.
■ Microwave: Not suitable.

RICOTTA CHEESE AND BACON PUFFS

2 bacon rashers, finely chopped
1 medium (150g) onion,
   finely chopped
3/4 cup (150g) ricotta cheese
3 eggs, lightly beaten
1/2 cup (75g) self-raising flour
1 tablespoon chopped fresh basil
vegetable oil for deep-frying
2 tablespoons finely grated
   parmesan cheese

Combine bacon and onion in pan, cook, stirring, until onion is soft; cool. Combine bacon mixture, ricotta, eggs, flour and basil in bowl.

Just before serving, drop tablespoons of mixture into hot oil in batches; cook until browned and puffed, drain on absorbent paper. Sprinkle with parmesan cheese.
Makes about 25.

■ Recipe best made just
  before serving.
■ Freeze: Not suitable.
■ Microwave: Not suitable.

ABOVE: Fried Cheese Triangles.
RIGHT: From back: Ricotta Cheese and Bacon Puffs; Crispy Prosciutto Hash Brown Patties.

Above: Platter from Corso De' Fiori; serviette ring from Pacific East India Co. Right: Tiles from Fred Pazotti.

SWEET SENSATIONS

The sweet treats presented here are bound to create a sensation, especially if they are an unexpected addition to the party. We have a tantalising array of delights to choose from – all in brilliant bite-sized portions. Consider chocolate, nuts and fruit in dreamy new ways; liqueur-laced creams and fillings; crisp pastries and crunchy biscotti; dainty meringues and petits fours. Everything has an innovative touch you'll love; many can be prepared or made ahead of time.

HEAVENLY RASPBERRY TUILES

Cook about 5 tuiles at a time until you become adept at handling them.

2 tablespoons caster sugar
1 egg white
1/4 cup (35g) plain flour
30g butter, melted
250g small fresh raspberries
small mint leaves

RASPBERRY FILLING
1/2 cup (60g) raspberries
1/4 cup (55g) caster sugar
2 teaspoons grated lemon rind
1 teaspoon lemon juice
1/2 cup (125g) mascarpone cheese

Cover the underside of an egg box with foil, pressing foil into crevices.

Combine sugar, egg white, flour and butter in bowl, stir until smooth; cover, stand at room temperature 30 minutes.

Mark 5 x 5cm circles on baking paper-covered oven trays, spread 1/2 teaspoons of mixture evenly into circles.

Bake in moderate oven about 3 minutes or until edges begin to colour. Slide a metal spatula under each tuile, quickly push tuile into the crevice of prepared egg box. Repeat with remaining mixture.

Just before serving, spoon raspberry filling into piping bag fitted with 7mm star tube, pipe filling into each tuile, top with a raspberry and mint leaf.

Raspberry Filling: Push raspberries through a fine sieve into bowl, stir in sugar, rind and juice. Whisk half the cheese into raspberry mixture, fold in remaining half. Refrigerate about 15 minutes or until thickened slightly.
Makes about 40.

■ Tuiles can be made a week ahead. Raspberry filling best made on day of serving.
■ Storage: Airtight container.
■ Freeze: Not suitable.
■ Microwave: Not suitable.

Heavenly Raspberry Tuiles.

China from Villeroy & Boch.

PEANUT BRITTLE

**2½ cups (375g) unsalted
  roasted peanuts**
¾ cup (165g) caster sugar
**1 cup (200g) firmly packed
  brown sugar**
½ cup (125ml) golden syrup
1 cup (250ml) water
60g butter
¼ teaspoon bicarbonate of soda

Spread nuts onto greased oven tray.
Combine sugars, golden syrup and
water in medium heavy-based pan, stir
over heat, without boiling, until sugar
dissolves. Add butter, boil, uncovered,
without stirring, until temperature
reaches 150°C on candy thermometer
(a teaspoon of mixture will snap when
dropped into a cup of cold water).
Mixture must not change colour. Allow
bubbles to subside, quickly stir in soda,
pour evenly over nuts; do not scrape
toffee from pan. Stand at room temperature to set. Break into pieces.

■ Recipe can be made 3 days ahead.
■ Storage: Airtight container.
■ Freeze: Not suitable.
■ Microwave: Not suitable.

LAMINGTON BITES

3 eggs
⅓ cup (75g) caster sugar
2 tablespoons cornflour
¼ cup (35g) plain flour
2 tablespoons self-raising flour
1 cup (90g) coconut, approximately
**⅔ cup (160ml) thickened cream,
  whipped**
**¼ cup (15g) shredded coconut,
  toasted**

ICING
3 cups (480g) icing sugar mixture
⅓ cup (35g) cocoa
10g butter, melted
½ cup (125ml) milk

Grease 23cm square slab cake pan,
place strip of baking paper to cover base
and extend over 2 opposite sides.

Beat eggs in medium bowl with
electric mixer until thick and creamy,
gradually beat in sugar, beating until
dissolved between each addition. Fold
in sifted flours, spread mixture into prepared pan. Bake cake in moderate
oven about 25 minutes; turn onto wire
rack to cool. Cut cake in half, cut each
half into 24 squares. Dip squares into
icing, drain away icing then toss
squares in coconut. Place lamingtons
on wire rack to set. Spoon cream into
piping bag fitted with small star tube.
Pipe a rosette of cream onto each lamington, decorate with shredded coconut.
Icing: Sift icing sugar and cocoa into
heatproof bowl, stir in butter and milk,
stir over pan of simmering water until
icing is of coating consistency.
Makes 48.

■ Cake best made a day ahead.
■ Storage: Airtight container.
■ Freeze: Lamingtons suitable,
  without cream.
■ Microwave: Icing suitable.

LEFT: Peanut Brittle.
BELOW: Lamington Bites.

Left: China from Accoutrement; tray from Mosmania.
Below: China from Home & Garden on the Mall.

PETITS FOURS

4 eggs
3/4 cup (165g) caster sugar
2/3 cup (100g) plain flour
1/3 cup (50g) cornflour
1/2 teaspoon baking powder
3/4 cup (180ml) apricot jam
2 tablespoons Frangelico
100g marzipan
500g packet prepared icing
1 egg white
1/2 cup (75g) Choc Melts, melted

Grease 26cm x 32cm Swiss roll pan, line with 2 sheets baking paper, extending 5cm above all sides of pan. In a small bowl, beat eggs with electric mixer about 7 minutes or until thick and creamy, gradually add sugar, beat until sugar dissolves. Gently fold in sifted dry ingredients. Pour mixture into prepared pan. Bake in moderate oven about 15 minutes. Cool in pan 5 minutes before turning onto wire rack to cool; remove paper.

Combine jam with liqueur in small pan; stir over heat until jam is melted; strain. Cut cake in half widthways; split each half horizontally.

Place 1 of the top layers of cake, topside down, onto tray, brush evenly with quarter of the jam mixture. Continue layering cake and jam mixture until all are used; the last layer of cake should be the base of sponge. Brush top of last cake layer with jam mixture.

Roll marzipan between sheets of baking paper to a 12cm x 21cm rectangle, place over cake; invert onto baking paper-covered tray. Top cake with baking paper, place another tray over paper; weight with a brick or other heavy object; refrigerate overnight.

Remove brick, tray and top piece of paper, invert cake onto board. Trim cake to measure 12cm x 21cm, cut cake into 3cm squares, place on wire rack with marzipan uppermost. Place icing in heatproof bowl over pan of simmering water, stir over heat until smooth. Add egg white, stir until

CHOCOLATE APRICOT LOGS

3/4 cup (110g) dried apricots
1/4 cup (60ml) boiling water
40g butter
2 tablespoons icing sugar mixture
1/4 cup (20g) coconut, toasted
1/2 cup (70g) slivered almonds,
toasted
1/4 cup (35g) White Melts, melted
1/3 cup (50g) Choc Melts, melted

Combine apricots and boiling water in heatproof bowl, cover, stand 1 hour. Drain apricots; discard liquid. Blend or process apricots with butter, icing sugar, coconut and almonds until combined. Wrap mixture in plastic; refrigerate overnight.

Shape rounded teaspoons of apricot mixture into 3cm logs, place on tray, refrigerate 30 minutes. Cut baking paper into 30 strips measuring 3cm x 8cm each. Spoon White Melts into piping bag fitted with small plain tube, pipe a pattern onto 1 strip of paper, stand until almost set, then spread Choc Melts evenly over the same paper strip. Immediately wrap paper around apricot log; stand until set.

Repeat with remaining strips of paper, Melts and apricot logs. Peel away paper when set.
Makes about 30.

■ Recipe can be made a week ahead.
■ Storage: Covered, in refrigerator.
■ Freeze: Not suitable.
■ Microwave: Chocolate suitable.

LEFT: Petits Fours.
BELOW: Chocolate Apricot Logs.

Left: Silver tray from Whitehill Silver; serviettes from Home & Garden on the Mall. Below: Cup and saucer from Accoutrement.

smooth; add a little water, if necessary, to bring icing to the consistency of pouring cream. Working quickly, pour icing over cakes on rack; spread icing around sides as each cake is iced. Ice as many cakes as possible, put back excess icing from tray into heatproof bowl, reheat over simmering water. Leave cakes to set at room temperature. Spoon chocolate into piping bag fitted with small plain tube, decorate petits fours with piped chocolate.
Makes 28.

■ Recipe can be made a day ahead.
■ Storage: Airtight container.
■ Freeze: Uniced layered cake suitable.
■ Microwave: Icing suitable.

HAZELNUT SUPREMES

1 cup (150g) plain flour
¼ cup (55g) caster sugar
60g butter, softened
2 egg yolks
2 teaspoons iced water

LIQUEUR FILLING
185g butter
½ cup (80g) icing sugar mixture
1 egg
¼ cup (60ml) Frangelico

TOPPING
15 toasted hazelnuts
¼ cup (35g) Choc Melts, melted

Process flour, sugar and butter until mixture resembles breadcrumbs; add egg yolks and water, process until ingredients cling together. Knead gently on lightly floured surface until smooth, cover; refrigerate 30 minutes.

Roll pastry between sheets of floured baking paper until 2mm thick. Cut pastry into 30 x 4.5cm rounds, press rounds into holes of mini muffin pans (1 tablespoon capacity). Lightly prick pastry bases with fork; refrigerate 30 minutes.

Bake in moderately hot oven about 10 minutes or until lightly browned; cool few minutes before removing pastry cases from pans; cool. Spoon liqueur filling into piping bag fitted with small star tube, pipe filling into cases. Top with hazelnuts and chocolate curls.

Liqueur Filling: Beat butter and icing sugar in small bowl with electric mixer until light and fluffy. Add egg and liqueur; beat until just combined.

Topping: Cut hazelnuts in half. Spread chocolate in thin layer over cool surface, such as granite or marble; allow to set at room temperature. Using large sharp knife, hold it at a 45° angle; pull gently over surface of chocolate to form curls. Makes 30.

■ Pastry cases, filling and chocolate curls can be made a day ahead.
■ Storage: Pastry cases, in airtight container. Filling and chocolate curls, covered, separately, in refrigerator.
■ Freeze: Baked pastry cases suitable.
■ Microwave: Choc Melts suitable.

ALMOND COCONUT MACAROONS

2 egg whites
⅔ cup (150g) caster sugar
1 cup (90g) coconut
½ cup (35g) shredded coconut
⅓ cup (40g) packaged ground almonds
2 egg whites, lightly beaten, extra
2 cups (160g) flaked almonds, chopped

In a small bowl, beat egg whites and sugar with electric mixer about 8 minutes or until sugar completely dissolves. Stir in coconuts and ground almonds; cover; refrigerate overnight.

Roll rounded teaspoons of mixture into 5cm logs, dip into extra egg whites, roll logs in flaked almonds. Place logs about 3cm apart on baking paper-covered oven trays. Bake in slow oven about 15 minutes or until macaroons are firm; cool on trays.
Makes about 50.

■ Recipe can be made a week ahead.
■ Storage: Airtight container.
■ Freeze: Suitable.
■ Microwave: Not suitable.

RIGHT: Almond Coconut Macaroons.
BELOW: Hazelnut Supremes.

Right: Glass bowl from Corso De' Fiori; cups from Villeroy & Boch. Below: China from Villeroy & Boch; glass from Opus Design.

RUM BALLS

**¼ cup (35g) finely chopped
  dried apricots**
2 tablespoons finely chopped raisins
**2 teaspoons finely chopped
  mixed peel**
1 tablespoon dark rum
¼ teaspoon ground ginger
¼ teaspoon ground cinnamon
**2 cups (200g) plain chocolate
  cake crumbs**
1 tablespoon cocoa
1 tablespoon marmalade
1 tablespoon dark rum, extra
**50g (½ cup) finely chopped amaretti
  macaroons**

Combine fruit, rum and spices in bowl, cover; stand 2 hours or overnight. Combine crumbs and sifted cocoa in bowl, stir in fruit mixture, marmalade and extra rum. Roll slightly rounded teaspoons of mixture in macaroons; shape into balls, place on tray, cover; refrigerate 3 hours.
Makes about 30.

■ Recipe can be made a week ahead.
■ Storage: Covered, in refrigerator.
■ Freeze: Not suitable.

LEMON MERINGUE KISSES

We used cream with a 54% fat content.

2 egg whites
½ cup (110g) caster sugar
2 teaspoons cornflour
½ teaspoon white vinegar
⅔ cup (160ml) bottled lemon butter
½ cup (125ml) cream

In a small bowl, beat egg whites with electric mixer until soft peaks form; gradually add sugar, beating until sugar is dissolved between each addition. Fold in cornflour and vinegar. Spoon meringue into piping bag fitted with 12mm plain tube. Pipe 3cm mounds of meringue about 2cm apart on baking paper-covered oven trays. Bake in very slow oven about 25 minutes or until meringues are firm and dry. Turn oven off, cool in oven with door ajar.

Just before serving, combine lemon butter and cream in bowl, spoon into piping bag fitted with small plain tube. Carefully make a small hole in base of meringues, pipe lemon butter cream mixture into meringues. Serve dusted with sifted icing sugar.

Makes about 35.

■ Meringues and filling can be
  made a day ahead.
■ Storage: Meringues, in airtight
  container. Filling, covered,
  in refrigerator.
■ Freeze: Not suitable.
■ Microwave: Not suitable.

LEFT: Rum Balls.
BELOW: Lemon Meringue Kisses.

Left: Glasses from Waterford Wedgwood.

CHOC ALMOND BITES

2 cups (280g) slivered almonds
3/4 cup (120g) icing sugar mixture
2 tablespoons Baileys Irish Cream
200g dark chocolate, melted
150g white chocolate, melted

Combine nuts, icing sugar and liqueur in large bowl; spread onto baking paper-covered oven tray. Bake in moderate oven, stirring occasionally, about 20 minutes or until sugar crystallises and mixture is grainy. Cool mixture on tray, stirring occasionally. Combine almond mixture and dark chocolate in bowl, mix well.

Drop rounded teaspoons of mixture onto baking paper-covered tray; refrigerate until set. Drizzle with white chocolate; refrigerate until set.
Makes about 45.

■ Recipe can be made 3 days ahead.
■ Storage: Covered, in refrigerator.
■ Freeze: Not suitable.
■ Microwave: Chocolate suitable.

CHOCOLATE PECAN BROWNIES

125g butter
1/2 cup (50g) cocoa
1/2 cup (125ml) milk
400g can sweetened condensed milk
2/3 cup (130g) firmly packed brown sugar
2 teaspoons vanilla essence
2/3 cup (100g) plain flour
2 eggs, lightly beaten
200g dark chocolate, chopped
1/4 cup (25g) pecans, toasted, chopped

Grease deep 23cm square cake pan; line base and sides with baking paper.

Combine butter, cocoa, milk and condensed milk in pan, whisk over low heat until smooth; transfer to large bowl. Stir in sugar, essence and sifted flour, then eggs; cool. Stir chocolate and nuts into milk mixture, spread into prepared pan. Bake in moderate oven about 30 minutes or until just firm.

Cool in pan; refrigerate until cold. Cut brownie into squares; dust with a little extra sifted cocoa, if preferred.
Makes about 25 squares.

■ Recipe can be made 3 days ahead.
■ Storage: Airtight container.
■ Freeze: Suitable.
■ Microwave: Not suitable.

ABOVE: Choc Almond Bites.
RIGHT: Chocolate Pecan Brownies

Above: China from Villeroy & Boch; tassel from Home & Garden on the Mall. Right: Sugar bowl from Home & Garden on the Mall.

ORANGE NUT BISCOTTI

½ cup (110g) caster sugar
1 egg
¾ cup (110g) plain flour
½ teaspoon baking powder
¾ cup (110g) macadamias,
  chopped, toasted
1 tablespoon cocoa
2 teaspoons grated orange rind

In a medium bowl, whisk sugar and egg together, stir in sifted flour and baking powder, then nuts; mix to a sticky dough. Divide dough in half. Knead sifted cocoa into 1 half, divide into 4 pieces; roll each piece into an 18cm log. On a lightly floured surface,

knead orange rind into remaining dough, divide in half; roll each piece into an 18cm log. Place 1 orange log on greased oven tray, place a chocolate log on each side, press logs gently together. Repeat with remaining logs, place on same tray. Bake logs in moderate oven about 30 minutes or until firm. Stand 10 minutes. Using a serrated knife, cut warm logs diagonally into 1cm slices. Place biscotti on oven trays. Bake in slow oven about 15 minutes or until dry and crisp.

Makes about 36.

■ Biscotti can be made a week ahead.
■ Storage: Airtight container.
■ Freeze: Not suitable.
■ Microwave: Not suitable.

SPICED CASHEW BISCOTTI

½ cup (110g) caster sugar
1 egg
¾ cup (110g) plain flour
½ teaspoon baking powder
1 teaspoon ground cinnamon
½ teaspoon ground cardamom
1 cup (150g) chopped unsalted
  roasted cashews

APRICOT-GLAZED CHEESECAKE CUPS

150g dark chocolate, melted
1/4 cup (60ml) apricot nectar
1 teaspoon gelatine
90g packaged cream cheese,
softened
2 tablespoons caster sugar
1 teaspoon lemon juice
1/4 cup (60ml) thickened cream

APRICOT GLAZE
2 teaspoons caster sugar
2 teaspoons arrowroot
1/3 cup (80ml) apricot nectar
1 teaspoon dark rum

Brush inside of foil confectionery cases with half the chocolate, refrigerate until set. Brush inside of cases again with remaining chocolate, refrigerate until set.

Peel foil cases away from chocolate. Place nectar in small pan, add gelatine, stir over low heat until gelatine is dissolved; cool. Beat cream cheese and sugar in small bowl with electric mixer until smooth; beat in juice and nectar mixture, fold in whipped cream. Spoon apricot mixture into chocolate cases; refrigerate until set. Spread apricot filling with apricot glaze; refrigerate until set. Top with candied rind, if preferred.

Apricot Glaze: Combine sugar and arrowroot in small pan, gradually stir in nectar and rum, stir over heat until mixture has thickened and become opaque; cool.

Makes about 40.

■ Recipe can be made a day ahead.
■ Storage: Covered, in refrigerator.
■ Freeze: Not suitable.
■ Microwave: Not suitable.

LEFT: From left: Orange Nut Biscotti;
Spiced Cashew Biscotti.
BELOW: Apricot-Glazed Cheesecake Cups.

In a medium bowl, whisk sugar and egg together, stir in sifted dry ingredients and nuts; mix to a sticky dough. Divide dough in half, shape each portion into an 18cm log on lightly floured surface. Place on greased oven tray, bake in moderate oven about 30 minutes or until firm. Stand 10 minutes. Using a serrated knife, cut warm logs diagonally into 1cm slices. Place biscotti on oven trays. Bake in slow oven about 15 minutes or until dry and crisp; cool on trays. Makes about 36.

■ Biscotti can be made a week ahead.
■ Storage: Airtight container.
■ Freeze: Not suitable.
■ Microwave: Not suitable.

PEPPERMINT COCONUT ICE

2½ cups (400g) pure icing sugar
¼ teaspoon cream of tartar
2 cups (180g) coconut
1 egg white
⅓ cup (80ml) sweetened
   condensed milk
green food colouring
peppermint essence

Line 8cm x 26cm bar pan with sheet of baking paper to cover base and extend over 2 opposite sides.

Sift icing sugar and cream of tartar into large bowl, add coconut, egg white and condensed milk; mix well. Press half the mixture firmly into prepared pan. Tint and flavour remaining mixture with colouring and essence, press over white layer, cover; refrigerate 3 hours. Remove coconut ice from pan, cut in half lengthways, cut each half into slices.
Makes about 50.

■ Recipe can be made 3 days ahead.
■ Storage: Covered, in refrigerator.
■ Freeze: Not suitable.

PANFORTE DI SIENA

2 sheets 15.5cm x 23.5cm rice paper
¾ cup (125g) brazil nuts, toasted
½ cup (80g) blanched
   almonds, toasted
½ cup (95g) chopped dried figs
½ cup (125g) chopped
   glace apricots
¼ cup (50g) glace ginger,
   finely chopped
⅓ cup (55g) chopped raisins
2 tablespoons cocoa
¼ cup (35g) plain flour
½ teaspoon ground nutmeg
½ teaspoon ground coriander
¼ teaspoon ground cloves
¼ cup (60ml) honey
¼ cup (55g) caster sugar
1 tablespoon water
1 tablespoon icing sugar mixture

Grease deep 17cm round cake pan, line base and side with baking paper. Cut half circles from each rice paper sheet to fit base of pan.

Combine nuts, fruit, sifted cocoa, flour and spices in bowl; mix well. Combine honey, caster sugar and water in small heavy-based pan, stir over heat until sugar dissolves, then boil, uncovered, without stirring, about 2 minutes or until temperature reaches 116°C on candy thermometer (a teaspoon of mixture will form a soft ball when dropped into a cup of cold water). Mixture must not change colour. Remove from heat, allow bubbles to subside, pour over nut mixture; mix well. Press mixture firmly into prepared pan. Bake in moderately slow oven about 45 minutes or until cake feels just firm; cool in pan. Remove cake from pan, wrap in foil; refrigerate overnight. Dust cake with sifted icing sugar; cut into thin wedges.
Serves about 20.

■ Recipe can be made a week ahead.
■ Storage: Covered, in refrigerator.
■ Freeze: Not suitable.
■ Microwave: Not suitable.

RIGHT: Panforte di Siena.
BELOW: Peppermint Coconut Ice.

Right: China from Waterford Wedgwood.
Below: Silver plate from Whitehill Silver; fabric from Boyac.

THREE-CHOCOLATE PRETZELS

1 cup (150g) plain flour
1/4 teaspoon ground cinnamon
1/4 cup (50g) brown sugar
60g butter, softened
2 egg yolks
2 teaspoons iced water,
    approximately
1 1/2 tablespoons vegetable oil
1/2 cup (75g) Choc Melts, melted
1/2 cup (75g) Milk Melts, melted
1/2 cup (75g) White Melts, melted

Combine flour, cinnamon, sugar and butter in processor, process about 30 seconds or until mixture resembles breadcrumbs; add egg yolks and enough water to make ingredients cling together. Knead gently on floured surface until smooth, cover; refrigerate 30 minutes.

LEFT: Three-Chocolate Pretzels.
ABOVE: Florentines.

Above: Heart-shaped plate and box from Morris Home & Garden Wares.

Roll slightly rounded teaspoons of dough into 17cm sausage shapes, shape into pretzels. Place pretzels about 3cm apart on greased oven trays. Bake in moderate oven about 12 minutes or until firm; cool on trays. Stir 2 teaspoons of the oil into each type of chocolate. Dip tops of 15 pretzels into each chocolate mixture, place on wire rack over tray, stand until set.
Makes about 45.

■ Pretzels can be made a week ahead.
■ Storage: Airtight container.
■ Freeze: Uniced pretzels suitable.
■ Microwave: Chocolate suitable.

FLORENTINES

1/2 cup (80g) sultanas
2 cups (60g) Corn Flakes
3/4 cup (105g) slivered
    almonds, chopped
1/2 cup (105g) glace cherries,
    finely chopped
2 tablespoons finely chopped
    glace ginger
2/3 cup (160ml) sweetened
    condensed milk
250g dark chocolate, melted

Combine sultanas, Corn Flakes, nuts, cherries, ginger and milk in large bowl. Drop rounded teaspoons of mixture about 2cm apart on baking paper-covered oven trays. Bake in moderate oven about 10 minutes or until browned; cool on trays. Spread base of each florentine with chocolate. Make wavy lines in chocolate with fork just before chocolate sets.
Makes about 50.

■ Recipe can be made 2 days ahead.
■ Storage: Airtight container.
■ Freeze: Not suitable.
■ Microwave: Chocolate suitable.

Truffles

All truffles can be made a week ahead and stored, covered, in the refrigerator. The icy chocolate pecan truffles are served frozen. However, none of the others is suitable to freeze. Each recipe makes about 40 truffles.

ICY CHOCOLATE PECAN

¼ cup (55g) caster sugar
2 egg yolks
⅓ cup (80ml) cream
125g dark chocolate, grated
1 tablespoon Grand Marnier
½ cup (60g) chopped pecans,
    toasted

Whisk sugar and egg yolks in small heatproof bowl until thick. Bring cream to boil in pan, gradually whisk hot cream into yolk mixture. Place bowl over pan of simmering water, stir over heat about 5 minutes or until custard thickens slightly. Remove from heat, add choco-late, stir until melted. Stir in liqueur, cover, freeze until mixture is firm. Roll teaspoons of mixture into balls, roll in pecans; freeze. Serve frozen.

RIGHT: Hazelnut and Irish Cream; Mandarin Pistachio; Brandied Peach; Lime and Malibu. BELOW: Icy Chocolate Pecan.

Right: China from Spode; tray from Whitehill Silver.
Below: China from Villeroy & Boch; serving bowl from Home & Garden on the Mall.

HAZELNUT AND IRISH CREAM

½ cup (125ml) cream
250g dark chocolate, finely chopped
3 teaspoons Baileys Irish Cream
⅓ cup (40g) finely chopped
    hazelnuts, toasted
250g Choc Melts, melted
50g White Melts, melted

Bring cream to the boil in small pan, pour over dark chocolate in bowl, stir until chocolate is melted. Stir in liqueur and nuts, cover; refrigerate, stirring occasionally, about 30 minutes or until mixture is thickened but not set.

Drop rounded teaspoons of mixture onto foil-covered tray, refrigerate about 15 minutes or until firm. Roll chocolate mixture into balls, refrigerate until firm. Dip truffles quickly in Choc Melts, gently and quickly roll between palms of hands to coat evenly, return to tray; refrigerate until set. Drizzle truffles with White Melts.

MANDARIN PISTACHIO

1/2 cup (125ml) cream
250g dark chocolate, finely chopped
3 teaspoons grated mandarin or
    orange rind
2 teaspoons Cointreau
1/4 cup (35g) finely chopped
    pistachios, toasted
250g Choc Melts, melted
20 pistachios, toasted, extra

Bring cream to the boil in small pan, pour over dark chocolate in bowl, stir until chocolate is melted. Stir in rind, liqueur and chopped nuts, cover; refrigerate, stirring occasionally, about 30 minutes or until mixture is thickened but not set.

Drop rounded teaspoons of mixture onto foil-covered tray; refrigerate about 15 minutes or until firm. Roll chocolate mixture into balls; refrigerate until firm. Dip truffles quickly in Choc Melts, gently and quickly roll between palms of hands to coat evenly, return to tray; refrigerate until set. Dip halved pistachios in a little chocolate, place on truffles.

BRANDIED PEACH

1/4 cup (60ml) cream
30g butter, chopped
250g White Melts, finely chopped
1/2 cup (125g) finely chopped
    glace peaches
3 teaspoons brandy
250g White Melts, melted, extra
1 glace peach, finely chopped, extra

Bring cream and butter to boil in small pan, pour over chopped White Melts in bowl, stir until chocolate is melted. Stir in peaches and brandy, cover; refrigerate, stirring occasionally, about 30 minutes or until mixture is thickened but not set.

Drop rounded teaspoons of mixture onto foil-covered tray; refrigerate about 15 minutes or until firm. Roll chocolate mixture into balls, refrigerate until firm. Dip truffles quickly in extra White Melts, gently and quickly roll between palms of hands to coat evenly, return to tray; refrigerate until set. Top with extra chopped glace peach.

LIME AND MALIBU

1/4 cup (60ml) cream
30g butter, chopped
250g White Melts, finely chopped
2 teaspoons grated lime rind
2 teaspoons Malibu
250g White Melts, melted, extra
50g Choc Melts, melted

Bring cream and butter to boil in small pan, pour over chopped White Melts in bowl, stir until chocolate is melted. Stir in rind and liqueur, cover; refrigerate, stirring occasionally, about 30 minutes or until mixture is thickened but not set.

Drop rounded teaspoons of mixture onto foil-covered tray, refrigerate 15 minutes or until firm. Roll chocolate mixture into balls, refrigerate until firm. Dip truffles quickly in extra White Melts, gently and quickly roll between palms of hands to coat evenly, return to tray; refrigerate until set. Spoon Choc Melts into piping bag fitted with small plain tube and decorate each truffle as preferred.

SPICED ALMOND DIAMONDS

250g packet plain sweet biscuits
125g butter, melted
1/3 cup (25g) flaked almonds

TOPPING
185g butter, softened
1 teaspoon vanilla essence
3/4 cup (165g) caster sugar
3 eggs
2 tablespoons plain flour
1/2 teaspoon ground cinnamon
1 1/2 cups (185g) packaged
ground almonds
1/4 cup (55g) chopped glace ginger
50g dark chocolate, grated

Crush biscuits finely, combine with butter in bowl. Press biscuit mixture over base of greased 20cm x 30cm lamington pan. Bake in moderate oven 10 minutes. Cool. Spread biscuit base with topping; sprinkle with almonds. Bake in moderate oven about 40 minutes or until set. Cool in pan. Cut slice into 6 strips lengthways, cut each strip into 5 diamonds; serve dusted with sifted icing sugar, if preferred.

Topping: Beat butter, essence and sugar in small bowl with electric mixer until thick and creamy. Add eggs 1 at a time, beat well between additions. Fold in sifted flour and cinnamon, almonds, ginger and chocolate.
Makes 30.

▨ Slice can be made a day ahead.
▨ Storage: Airtight container.
▨ Freeze: Not suitable.
▨ Microwave: Not suitable.

MINI MOCHACCINOS

1 1/4 cups (185g) Milk Melts, melted
3/4 cup (185ml) mascarpone cheese
1 tablespoon Kahlua
200g packet coffee thins
drinking chocolate

Using a small paint brush, paint about 1 cup melted Milk Melts all over insides of 30 foil confectionery cases; refrigerate until set. Peel foil cases away from chocolate. Spoon remaining Milk Melts into piping bag fitted with small plain tube. Pipe 30 x 1cm long semi-circles onto sheet of baking paper (to look like cup handles), allow to set. Attach handles to cups using more Milk Melts. Combine mascarpone and Kahlua in small bowl; divide among cups. Place cups on top of coffee thins, dust with a little sifted drinking chocolate.
Makes 30.

▨ Recipe can be made 3 days ahead.
▨ Storage: Covered, in refrigerator.
▨ Freeze: Not suitable.
▨ Microwave: Chocolate suitable.

LEFT: Spiced Almond Diamonds.
BELOW: Mini Mochaccinos.

Left: China from Royal Worcester; tea strainer from Home & Garden on the Mall. Below: Placemat from Home & Garden on the Mall.

SUGARED JELLIES

2 tablespoons gelatine
3/4 cup (180ml) water
2 cups (440g) caster sugar
3/4 cup (180ml) apple juice
1 tablespoon lemon juice
2 teaspoons grated lime rind
green food colouring
1/4 cup (55g) sugar

Line base and sides of 8cm x 26cm bar pan with foil; grease foil.

Sprinkle gelatine over water in bowl, stand 5 minutes. Combine caster sugar and apple juice in pan, stir over heat, without boiling, until sugar dissolves; simmer, uncovered, without stirring, about 15 minutes or until temperature reaches 122°C on candy thermometer (a teaspoon of mixture will form a hard ball when dropped into a cup of cold water). Mixture must not change colour. Remove from heat, allow bubbles to subside. Stir in gelatine mixture, lemon juice and rind. Tint mixture green with colouring, pour into prepared pan; cool. Refrigerate jelly until firm. Cut jelly into 2cm squares, place cubes on wire rack, stand, uncovered, at least 12 hours. Toss jelly cubes in sugar.
Makes about 50.

■ Sugared jellies can be made 2 days ahead.
■ Storage: Airtight container.
■ Freeze: Not suitable.
■ Microwave: Not suitable.

RIGHT: Orange Poppy Seed Shortbread.
BELOW: Sugared Jellies.

Right: China from Waterford Wedgwood; tea-towel from The Bay Tree Kitchen Shop. Below: Platter from Corso De' Fiori.

ORANGE POPPY SEED SHORTBREAD

250g butter, softened
1 tablespoon grated orange rind
1/4 cup (55g) caster sugar
2 teaspoons orange juice
1 tablespoon poppy seeds
1½ cups (225g) plain flour

In a small bowl, beat butter, rind and sugar with electric mixer until light and fluffy. Stir in juice, seeds and sifted flour in 2 batches. Spoon mixture into piping bag fitted with small star tube. Pipe 3cm shapes about 2cm apart onto greased oven trays. Bake in moderate oven about 12 minutes or until lightly browned. Stand shortbread on trays 2 minutes before transferring to wire rack to cool.
Makes about 70.

■ Recipe can be made a week ahead.
■ Storage: Airtight container.
■ Freeze: Not suitable.
■ Microwave: Not suitable.

COCONUT CHERRY CHOCOLATE TRIANGLES

125g butter, melted
2 cups (320g) icing sugar mixture
¼ cup (60ml) thickened cream
¼ cup (50g) glace cherries,
  finely chopped
2 cups (180g) coconut
red food colouring
375g dark chocolate, chopped
30g butter, extra

Line base and sides of 20cm x 30cm lamington pan with foil; grease foil.

Combine butter, icing sugar, cream, cherries and coconut in bowl; mix well; tint pink with colouring. Combine choco-late and extra butter in heatproof bowl over simmering water, stir until smooth. Spread half chocolate mixture over base of prepared pan; refrigerate until set.

Press coconut mixture gently over chocolate in pan, refrigerate until firm. Reheat remaining chocolate mixture over simmering water, spread over coconut mixture, cover; refrigerate 2 hours. Cut slice into 4cm x 5cm rectangles; cut each in half diagonally.
Makes 60.

▨ Recipe can be made 3 days ahead.
▨ Storage: Covered, in refrigerator.
▨ Freeze: Not suitable.
▨ Microwave: Not suitable.

LEMON CURD TARTLETS

90g butter
¼ cup (55g) caster sugar
1 egg, lightly beaten
1¼ cups (185g) plain flour
¼ cup (35g) self-raising flour

FILLING
2 eggs
⅓ cup (75g) caster sugar
2 teaspoons grated lemon rind
¼ cup (60ml) lemon juice
40g butter

LEMON SHREDS
1 medium (140g) lemon
½ cup (110g) caster sugar
¼ cup (60ml) water

In a small bowl, beat butter with electric mixer until just smooth. Add sugar and egg, beat only until combined; do not overbeat. Stir in half the sifted flours, work in remaining flours with fingers. Knead pastry gently on lightly floured surface until smooth, cover; refrigerate 30 minutes.

Roll pastry between sheets of baking paper until 2mm thick. Cut into 5.5cm fluted rounds, press into 4 x 12 hole shallow patty pan trays, cover; refrigerate 30 minutes. Lightly prick pastry bases with fork. Bake in moderately hot oven about 10 minutes or until lightly browned; cool. Spoon filling into cases; top with lemon shreds.

Filling: Whisk eggs in heatproof bowl until frothy, whisk in sugar, rind and juice. Add butter, stir constantly over pan of simmering water until mixture thickens slightly. Remove from heat, cover; refrigerate until cold.

Lemon Shreds: Using a vegetable peeler, peel rind thinly from lemon. Cut rind into very thin strips. Combine sugar and water in small pan, stir over heat, without boiling, until sugar dissolves. Add rind, simmer, uncovered, about 5 minutes or until mixture is syrupy. Remove rind from syrup, place on greased tray, separate strips of rind.

Makes about 48.

■ Pastry cases, filling and lemon shreds can be made a day ahead.
■ Storage: Pastry cases, in airtight container. Filling and lemon shreds covered, separately, in refrigerator.
■ Freeze: Baked pastry cases suitable.
■ Microwave: Not suitable.

ABOVE: Coconut Cherry Chocolate Triangles.
LEFT: Lemon Curd Tartlets.

Above: China from Waterford Wedgwood. Left: China from Villeroy & Boch.

CHOCOLATE PISTACHIO ROLLS

200g dark chocolate, chopped
1/3 cup (80ml) cream
2 teaspoons brandy
2 teaspoons instant coffee powder
1/3 cup (50g) chopped pistachios, toasted
250g marzipan
1 tablespoon apricot jam, warmed
200g Choc Melts, melted
2 teaspoons vegetable oil

Combine chocolate and cream in small heatproof bowl, place over pan of simmering water, stir until smooth. Stir in brandy, coffee and nuts, cover; refrigerate until firm.

Divide chocolate mixture in half, roll each half between sheets of plastic wrap to form 28cm sausage shapes; refrigerate until firm. Divide marzipan in half, roll each half between sheets of baking paper to 11cm x 28cm rectangles, spread with jam. Top each with a chocolate log. Roll marzipan over to enclose logs; trim edges so they meet neatly; refrigerate until firm.

Brush each log with combined Choc Melts and oil, so that marzipan is thickly coated in chocolate. Place on baking paper-covered tray; allow to set at room temperature. Trim ends from logs, cut diagonally into 1cm slices.

Makes about 50.

- Recipe can be made 3 days ahead.
- Storage: Covered, in refrigerator.
- Freeze: Not suitable.
- Microwave: Chocolate mixture suitable.

PASSIONFRUIT POWDER PUFFS

You will need about 4 passionfruit for this recipe.

1 egg
1/4 cup (55g) caster sugar
2 tablespoons cornflour
2 tablespoons plain flour

PASSIONFRUIT FILLING
1/2 cup (125ml) thickened cream
250g mascarpone cheese
2 tablespoons icing sugar mixture
1/3 cup (80ml) passionfruit pulp

In a small bowl, beat egg with electric mixer on high speed 1 minute; gradually add sugar, continue beating on medium speed about 10 minutes or until mixture is thick enough to hold its shape. Sift flours over egg mixture, fold through gently until just combined. Drop teaspoons of mixture about 4cm apart onto greased oven trays (allow 6 puffs per tray). Bake in moderate oven about 10 minutes or until puffs are lightly browned. Using a metal spatula, remove puffs immediately from tray to a wire rack to cool.

Just before serving, spread or pipe passionfruit filling onto flat side of half the puffs, top with remaining puffs. Dust with sifted icing sugar, if preferred.

Passionfruit Filling: Beat cream in small bowl with electric mixer until slightly thickened, add cheese and icing sugar, beat until thick; fold in passionfruit.

Makes about 24.

- Recipe best made on day of serving.
- Storage: Filling, covered, in refrigerator.
- Freeze: Not suitable.
- Microwave: Not suitable.

LEFT: Chocolate Pistachio Rolls.
BELOW: Passionfruit Powder Puffs.

MACADAMIA MAPLE NOUGAT

This delicious nougat recipe needs to be followed carefully. It is advisable to use a candy thermometer for accuracy, and it is important to work quickly during preparation. We used a mixer on a stand.

3 sheets (15.5cm x 23.5cm) rice paper
2 cups (440g) caster sugar
1 cup (250ml) glucose syrup
½ cup (125ml) maple syrup
1 teaspoon vanilla essence
2 egg whites
75g butter, softened
1½ cups (225g) macadamias,
toasted

Grease 19cm x 29cm rectangular slice pan. Trim 1½ sheets of rice paper to fit base of pan.

Combine sugar, syrups and essence in medium heavy-based pan, stir over low heat, without boiling, until sugar dissolves. Bring to boil, boil rapidly, without stirring, about 6 minutes, or until temperature reaches 138°C (small crack stage) on candy thermometer (a teaspoon of mixture will snap when dropped into a cup of cold water). Remove from heat.

Meanwhile, beat egg whites in small bowl with electric mixer until firm peaks form. Transfer egg whites to large bowl. With mixer operating, gradually pour in hot syrup mixture in a thin steady stream, beat about 3 minutes or until mixture is very thick and holds its shape.

Add butter, beat about 1 minute or until butter is combined and mixture very thick; stir in nuts. Spread immediately into prepared pan, cover with piece of well-greased foil. Using the foil as a barrier, take a plastic spatula and smooth the top of nougat; remove foil. Trim remaining rice paper to fit over nougat, press rice paper onto nougat. Cool to room temperature (this will take about 6 hours). Turn nougat out of pan. Using oiled knife, trim edges, cut into 3cm squares.
Makes 54.

■ Recipe can be made 2 weeks ahead.
■ Storage: Airtight container in a cool, dry place.
■ Freeze: Not suitable.
■ Microwave: Not suitable.

RIGHT: Fruit and Nut Clusters.
BELOW: Macadamia Maple Nougat.

Below: China from Waterford Wedgwood.

FRUIT AND NUT CLUSTERS

½ cup (80g) chopped dates
½ cup (75g) chopped dried apricots
½ cup (75g) macadamias, toasted, chopped
½ cup (75g) hazelnuts, toasted, chopped
375g packet White Melts, melted
1½ cups (105g) shredded coconut, toasted

Combine fruits and nuts in large bowl, stir in chocolate. Drop heaped teaspoons of mixture into coconut; shape into balls, place on foil-covered trays. Refrigerate until set.
Makes about 60.

■ Clusters can be made 3 days ahead.
■ Storage: Covered, in refrigerator.
■ Freeze: Not suitable.
■ Microwave: Chocolate suitable.

APRICOT ALMOND BREAD

2 egg whites
1/3 cup (75g) caster sugar
3/4 cup (110g) plain flour
1/4 teaspoon ground cinnamon
1/4 teaspoon ground nutmeg
1/4 teaspoon ground ginger
1/3 cup (55g) almond kernels
1/3 cup (50g) pistachios
1/2 cup (75g) chopped dried apricots

Grease 8cm x 26cm bar pan, line base and sides with baking paper.

In a small bowl, beat egg whites and sugar with electric mixer about 8 minutes or until sugar dissolves and mixture thickens. Fold in sifted dry ingredients, nuts and apricots; spread into prepared pan. Bake in moderate oven about 30 minutes or until lightly browned. Cool in pan, wrap in foil; stand overnight.

Using serrated knife, slice bread very thinly. Place slices on baking paper-covered oven trays, bake in slow oven about 20 minutes or until dry and crisp. Makes about 70.

▨ Recipe can be made a week ahead.
▨ Storage: Airtight container.
▨ Freeze: Unsliced bread suitable.
▨ Microwave: Not suitable.

COFFEE CREAMS

1 1/4 cups (185g) White Melts, melted
1 egg yolk
1/3 cup (55g) icing sugar mixture
60g unsalted butter
125g dark chocolate, melted
1 teaspoon instant coffee powder
1 teaspoon water
2 teaspoons Tia Maria or Kahlua

Brush inside of foil confectionery cases, using about half the White Melts; refrigerate until set. Repeat process. Use remaining White Melts (melt again, if necessary) to pipe 1.5cm squiggles onto sheet of baking paper; refrigerate until set.

Meanwhile, whisk egg yolk and icing sugar in small heatproof bowl over simmering water until thick, cover; cool. Beat butter in small bowl with electric mixer until as white as possible; beat in egg mixture, cooled chocolate and combined coffee, water and liqueur.

Peel foil cases away from chocolate. Spoon coffee cream into piping bag fitted with medium star tube, pipe into chocolate cases; top with chocolate squiggles; refrigerate about 30 minutes or until filling has set.
Makes about 25.

▨ Recipe can be made a day ahead.
▨ Storage: Covered, in refrigerator.
▨ Freeze: Not suitable.
▨ Microwave: Not suitable.

ABOVE: Apricot Almond Bread.
RIGHT: Coffee Creams.

Above: Plate from Accoutrement. Right: China from Orson & Blake Collectables.

FRESH FRUITS WITH LIQUEUR CREAM AND PRALINE

Any variety of seasonal fruit can be used for the fruit platter. For liqueur cream and praline, any combination of liqueur and nuts can be used, such as Frangelico with hazelnuts, Kahlua with cashews, Cointreau with macadamias, Amaretto with almonds, or Creme de Cacao with brazil nuts.

250g strawberries
3 medium (330g) tamarillos, quartered
3 medium (180g) figs, quartered
10 (230g) fresh dates, seeded
2 medium (230g) carambola, sliced
2 medium (460g) pears, cored, sliced
3 medium (255g) kiwi fruit, quartered

LIQUEUR CREAM
2 cups (500g) mascarpone cheese
1/4 cup (60ml) liqueur
2 tablespoons icing sugar mixture

PRALINE
3/4 cup nuts, toasted
2/3 cup (150g) caster sugar
1/3 cup (80ml) water

Arrange fruit on platter, serve with liqueur cream and praline.
Liqueur Cream: Beat cheese, liqueur and sifted icing sugar in small bowl with electric mixer until smooth.
Praline: Place nuts on greased oven tray. Combine sugar and water in small heavy-based pan, stir over heat, without boiling, until sugar dissolves. Boil rapidly, uncovered, without stirring, until lightly browned. Pour toffee mixture over nuts; leave to set. When cold, blend or process until praline is finely chopped.
Serves 10 to 12.

▓ Fruit best cut just before serving. Praline can be made a week ahead. Liqueur cream can be made a day ahead.
▓ Storage: Liqueur cream, covered, in refrigerator. Praline, in airtight container.
▓ Freeze: Not suitable.
▓ Microwave: Not suitable.

RICH CHOC CRACKLES

100g Copha
1/2 cup (80g) icing sugar mixture
2 1/2 cups (85g) Rice Bubbles
1/3 cup (30g) coconut
50g dark chocolate, melted
1/3 cup (35g) cocoa
25g butter, melted

Melt Copha in large pan over low heat; cool 15 minutes. Fold in remaining ingredients gently in 2 batches. Drop rounded teaspoons of mixture into small paper patty cases, top with sweets, if preferred; refrigerate until set.
Makes about 55.

▓ Recipe can be made 3 days ahead.
▓ Storage: Covered, in refrigerator.
▓ Freeze: Not suitable.
▓ Microwave: Not suitable.

LEFT: Fresh Fruits with Liqueur Cream and Praline.
BELOW: Rich Choc Crackles.

Left: Glass bowls and champagne flutes from H.A.G. Imports.

BRANDIED-FRUIT CRESCENTS

1⅓ cups (200g) self-raising flour
⅓ cup (40g) packaged
　ground almonds
1 teaspoon ground cinnamon
⅓ cup (75g) caster sugar
80g butter, chopped
1 egg, lightly beaten
¼ cup (60ml) sour cream

FILLING
¼ cup (35g) finely chopped
　dried apricots
1 tablespoon brandy
2 tablespoons bottled fruit mince

Sift flour into bowl, add nuts, cinnamon and sugar; rub in butter. Stir in egg and cream, then knead pastry gently on a floured surface until smooth (or process flour, nuts, cinnamon, sugar and butter until mixture resembles breadcrumbs; add egg and cream, process until mixture forms a ball). Divide mixture into quarters, cover; refrigerate 20 minutes.

Roll each piece of pastry into 20cm round on floured surface. Cut each round into 8 wedges. Place ½ teaspoon of filling at wide edge of wedges, roll up wedges, from filling edge, to form crescents. Place crescents about 2cm apart on greased oven trays. Bake in moderately hot oven about 10 minutes or until lightly browned. Cool on trays. Serve crescents dusted with sifted icing sugar.

Filling: Combine apricots and brandy in bowl, cover; stand 1 hour. Combine apricot mixture with fruit mince in bowl.

Makes 32.

▨ Recipe can be made 3 days ahead.
▨ Storage: Airtight container.
▨ Freeze: Suitable.
▨ Microwave: Not suitable.

RIGHT: Orange Liqueur Chocolate Tartlets.
BELOW: Brandied-Fruit Crescents.

Below: China from Waterford Wedgwood.

ORANGE LIQUEUR CHOCOLATE TARTLETS

1¼ cups (185g) plain flour
¼ cup (25g) cocoa
125g cold butter, chopped
1 egg yolk
1 tablespoon iced water,
   approximately

FILLING
300ml thickened cream
1⅔ cups (250g) White Melts
2 tablespoons Grand Marnier
1 tablespoon grated orange rind

CANDIED RIND
1 medium (180g) orange
½ cup (110g) caster sugar
¼ cup (60ml) water

Sift flour and cocoa into bowl, rub in butter, add egg yolk and enough water to make ingredients cling together (or make pastry in processor). Press dough into a ball, knead gently on lightly floured surface until smooth, cover; refrigerate 30 minutes.

Divide pastry in half. Roll each half between sheets of baking paper until 1mm thick. Cut pastry into 5cm fluted rounds, press rounds into 5 x 12 hole tiny tartlet trays (3 teaspoon capacity), prick pastry bases with skewer; refrigerate 30 minutes. Bake pastry cases in moderately hot oven about 7 minutes or until crisp; cool. Spoon filling into piping bag fitted with small star tube. Pipe filling into pastry cases; top with candied rind.
Filling: Heat cream in small pan until boiling, pour over White Melts in bowl, stir until White Melts have melted. Stir in

liqueur and rind; refrigerate until firm. Beat mixture with electric mixer until fluffy; do not over-beat (mixture should resemble whipped cream).
Candied Rind: Using a vegetable peeler, peel rind thinly from orange. Cut rind into very thin strips. Combine sugar and water in small pan, stir over heat, without boiling, until sugar dissolves. Add rind, simmer, uncovered, about 5 minutes or until mixture is syrupy. Remove rind from syrup, place on greased tray, separate strips of rind.
Makes about 60.

■ Pastry cases and candied rind can be made a day ahead.
■ Storage: Separately, in airtight containers.
■ Freeze: Cooked pastry cases suitable.
■ Microwave: Not suitable.

115

PISTACHIO CARAMEL LOGS

125g butter, chopped
400g can sweetened condensed milk
2 tablespoons golden syrup
**¾ cup (150g) firmly packed
    brown sugar**
½ teaspoon cream of tartar
**¾ cup (110g) pistachios, toasted,
    finely chopped**

Line base and sides of deep 19cm square cake pan with baking paper.

Combine butter, milk, golden syrup, sugar and cream of tartar in medium heavy-based pan, stir over heat, without boiling, until sugar dissolves. Bring to boil, whisk constantly over heat about 8 minutes or until mixture is thick and dark caramel in colour. Pour mixture into prepared pan; do not scrape mixture from pan. Stand caramel 15 minutes. Mark 6 strips in caramel with a greased knife; cool. Remove caramel from pan, cut into strips where marked. Roll strips in nuts, shaping each into a 32cm long sausage; press nuts firmly into caramel. Cut diagonally into 4cm pieces.
Makes about 48.

■ Recipe can be made a week ahead.
■ Storage: Covered, in refrigerator.
■ Freeze: Not suitable.
■ Microwave: Not suitable.

CARAMEL WAFER BISCUITS

We used Belgian Butters for wafers in this recipe.

400g can sweetened condensed milk
50g butter
2 tablespoons maple syrup
25 packaged wafer crisps
¼ cup (35g) Choc Melts, melted
1 teaspoon vegetable oil

BRAZIL NUT PRALINE
¼ cup (55g) caster sugar
¼ cup (60ml) water
**2 tablespoons chopped brazil nuts,
    toasted**

Combine milk, butter and maple syrup in medium heavy-based pan, whisk constantly over medium heat about 6 minutes or until mixture is thick and darker in colour; stand at room temperature until warm.

Brush half of one side of wafer crisps with combined Choc Melts and oil; allow to set on wire rack. Spoon caramel mixture into piping bag fitted with medium star tube, pipe onto wafer crisps; sprinkle with brazil nut praline.
Brazil Nut Praline: Combine sugar and water in small pan, stir over heat, without boiling, until sugar dissolves. Boil, uncovered, without stirring, until lightly browned; add nuts, do not stir, pour onto greased oven tray. When praline is set, chop finely.
Makes 25.

■ Recipe can be made 3 hours ahead.
■ Storage: Covered loosely in a cool,
    dry place.
■ Freeze: Not suitable.
■ Microwave: Chocolate suitable.

LEFT: Pistachio Caramel Logs.
BELOW: Caramel Wafer Biscuits.

Left: Serviette ring from Pacific East India Co.
Below: Setting from Morris Home & Garden Wares.

MARSHMALLOW FUDGE DOMINOES

100g packet pink marshmallows
30g butter
1 tablespoon water
250g white chocolate, chopped
100g packet white
  marshmallows, extra
30g butter, extra
1 tablespoon water, extra
250g white chocolate, chopped, extra

Line base and sides of 8cm x 26cm bar pan with baking paper. Combine pink marshmallows, butter and water in medium pan, stir over low heat until marshmallows are melted. Remove from heat, add chocolate, stir vigorously until chocolate is melted and mixture thick, pour into prepared pan. Tap pan on bench to remove air bubbles; refrigerate 1 hour.

Make white layer, following instructions above, and using remaining ingredients. Cover; refrigerate 3 hours before cutting into small pieces.

Makes about 64.

■ Recipe can be made a week ahead.
■ Storage: Covered, in refrigerator.
■ Freeze: Not suitable.
■ Microwave: Suitable.

SPICED BOW TIES

2 eggs
2 tablespoons caster sugar
1¼ cups (185g) plain flour
½ teaspoon ground ginger
vegetable oil for deep-frying
2 tablespoons cinnamon sugar
2 tablespoons icing sugar mixture

Blend or process eggs, sugar, flour and ginger until mixture resembles breadcrumbs. Knead gently on lightly floured surface until smooth, cover; refrigerate 2 hours.

Roll mixture between sheets of baking paper until 2mm thick. Cut into 4cm fluted squares, pinch squares together in centre to resemble bows. Deep-fry bows in hot oil in batches until lightly browned; drain, sprinkle with cinnamon sugar. Just before serving, dust with icing sugar.

Makes about 45.

■ Recipe can be made a day ahead.
■ Storage: Airtight container.
■ Freeze: Not suitable.
■ Microwave: Not suitable.

ABOVE: Marshmallow Fudge Dominoes.
RIGHT: Spiced Bow Ties.

Above: China from The Bay Tree Kitchen Shop. Right:
Setting from Orson & Blake Collectables.

TOFFEE-TOPPED PROFITEROLES

40g butter, chopped
½ cup (125ml) water
½ cup (75g) plain flour
2 eggs

FILLING
300ml thickened cream
2 tablespoons Cointreau
1 tablespoon icing sugar mixture

TOFFEE
¾ cup (165g) sugar
¼ cup (60ml) water

Combine butter and water in pan, stir over heat until butter has melted and mixture boils. Add flour all at once, stir vigorously over heat until mixture leaves side of pan. Transfer mixture to small bowl of electric mixer. Beat in eggs 1 at a time, beat on low speed until smooth. Drop teaspoons of mixture 3cm apart onto greased oven trays. Bake in moderately hot oven 10 minutes. Reduce heat to moderate, bake further 5 minutes or until profiteroles are lightly browned. Cool on wire rack. Cut each profiterole in half, remove any soft centres.

Just before serving, join profiteroles with filling; place on wire rack over tray and drizzle toffee over top of profiteroles.

Filling: Beat all ingredients in small bowl with electric mixer until thick.
Toffee: Combine sugar and water in small heavy-based pan, stir over heat, without boiling, until sugar is dissolved. Boil, uncovered, without stirring, until mixture is golden brown.
Makes about 60.

- Profiteroles and filling can be made a day ahead.
- Storage: Profiteroles, in airtight container. Filling, covered, in refrigerator.
- Freeze: Unfilled profiteroles suitable.
- Microwave: Not suitable.

BRANDY SNAP CIGARS

Cook about 6 snaps at a time until you become adept at handling them.

50g butter
⅓ cup (65g) firmly packed brown sugar
⅓ cup (80ml) golden syrup
½ teaspoon ground ginger
½ cup (75g) plain flour
⅔ cup (100g) White Melts, melted

FILLING
300ml sour cream
1 tablespoon caster sugar
2 tablespoons Baileys Irish Cream

Combine butter, sugar, golden syrup and ginger in medium pan, stir over low heat, without boiling, until butter is melted. Remove from heat, stir in sifted flour. Drop ½ teaspoons of mixture about 6cm apart on greased oven trays. Bake in moderate oven about 6 minutes or until snaps are bubbling and lightly browned. Working quickly, slide a metal spatula under each snap, wrap quickly around the handle of a wooden spoon. Remove snap from spoon handle, place on wire rack to firm.

Just before serving, spoon filling into piping bag fitted with small star tube, pipe filling into brandy snaps; drizzle with White Melts.
Filling: Beat cream, sugar and liqueur in small bowl with electric mixer until firm peaks form.
Makes about 60.

- Snaps can be made a week ahead. Filling best made on day of serving.
- Storage: Snaps, in airtight container.
- Freeze: Not suitable.
- Microwave: Not suitable.

LEFT: Toffee-Topped Profiteroles.
BELOW: Brandy Snap Cigars.

Below: China from Waterford Wedgwood.

Glossary

Here are some terms, names and alternatives to help everyone use and understand our recipes perfectly.

AMARETTO: an almond-flavoured liqueur.

ARROWROOT: used mostly for thickening. Cornflour can be substituted.

BACON RASHERS: bacon slices.

BAILEYS IRISH CREAM: an Irish whiskey-based liqueur with cream added.

BAKING POWDER: a raising agent consisting of a starch, but mostly cream of tartar and bicarbonate of soda in the proportions of 1 level teaspoon of cream of tartar to 1/2 level teaspoon bicarbonate of soda. This is equivalent to 2 teaspoons of baking powder.

BEETROOT: regular round beet.

BICARBONATE OF SODA: baking soda.

BREADCRUMBS:
Packaged: use fine packaged crumbs.
Stale: use 1- or 2-day-old bread made into crumbs by grating, blending or processing.

BUTTER: use salted or unsalted (also called sweet) butter; 125g is equal to 1 stick butter.

BUTTERMILK: made by adding a culture to a low-fat milk to give a slightly acidic flavour; a low-fat milk can be substituted.

CABANOSSI: a sausage made from a mixture of smoked pork and beef that needs no cooking; also known as cabana.

CAJUN SEASONING: dried mixture consisting of salt, peppers, garlic, onion and spices.

CARAMBOLA: star fruit, yellow in colour with waxy skin and crisp, juicy flesh. Can be eaten fresh or used in desserts.

CHEESE:
Baked ricotta: ricotta cheese slowly baked to create a firmer, drier cheese than the fresh ricotta.
Bocconcini: small balls of mild, delicate cheese packaged in water or whey to keep them white and soft.
Cream: also known as Philly.
Feta: a soft Greek cheese with a sharp, salty taste.
Goats': made from goats' milk.
Gruyere: a Swiss cheese with small holes and a nutty flavour.

Light cream: made from a blend of cottage and cream cheese, with a minimum fat content of 14 per cent.
Mascarpone: a fresh, unripened, smooth triple-cream cheese with a rich sweet taste; slightly acidic.
Mozzarella: a fresh, semi-soft cheese with a delicate, clean, fresh curd taste; has a stringy texture when heated.
Parmesan: sharp-tasting hard cheese used as a flavour accent.
Quark (baker's cheese): is similar to cottage cheese with a mild acidic flavour.
Ricotta: fresh, unripened, light curd cheese.
Smoked: use a firm smoked cheese.
Soft cream: a spreadable cream cheese; do not confuse with light cream cheese.
Tasty cheddar: matured cheddar; use a hard, good-tasting variety.

CHICKEN SALT: consists of salt, onion, pepper, red pepper and spices; used to flavour chicken.

CHICKPEAS: garbanzos.
Roasted: available from health food stores, ready to eat when bought.

CHILLIES: available in different types and sizes. Use rubber gloves when chopping fresh chillies as they can burn your skin.

CHORIZO: spicy sausage made with pork.

COCONUT: use desiccated coconut, unless otherwise specified.
Cream: available in cans and cartons.
Flaked: flaked dried coconut flesh.
Milk: available in cans.
Shredded: thin strips of dried coconut.

COFFEE THINS: milk and dark chocolate discs, about 5cm wide.

COINTREAU: orange-flavoured liqueur.

COPHA: a solid white shortening based on coconut oil. Kremelta and Palmin can be substituted.

CORNFLOUR: cornstarch.

COUSCOUS: a fine cereal made from semolina.

CREAM: fresh pouring cream; has a minimum fat content of 35 per cent.
Low fat sour cream: commercially cultured soured cream; not as firm as sour cream. It contains 18 per cent fat.
Sour: a thick, commercially cultured soured cream containing not less than 35 per cent fat.
Thickened (whipping): has a minimum fat content of 35 per cent and contains a thickener.

CREAM OF TARTAR: an acid which acts with an alkali as a raising agent in flour; it is one of the ingredients in baking powder.

DRINKING CHOCOLATE: sweetened cocoa powder.

ESSENCE: extract.

FILLO PASTRY: also known as phyllo dough; comes in tissue-thin pastry sheets bought chilled or frozen.

FISH SAUCE: made from liquid drained from salted, fermented anchovies. Has a strong smell and taste; use sparingly. We used Thai fish sauce in this book.

FIVE SPICE POWDER: a pungent mixture of ground spices which includes cinnamon, cloves, fennel, star anise and Szechwan peppers.

FLOUR:
Chickpea: made from ground chickpeas; also known as gram or besan flour.
Plain: all-purpose flour.
Self-raising: substitute plain (all-purpose) flour and baking powder in the proportions of 1 cup (150g) plain flour to 2 level teaspoons baking powder. Sift together several times before using.

Shredded coconut

Flaked coconut

Desiccated coconut

Wholemeal self-raising: wholewheat self-raising flour; add baking powder to make wholemeal self-raising flour.

FRANGELICO: a hazelnut-flavoured liqueur.

FRENCH GOURMET HERBS (DRIED): a mixture of parsley, chervil, tarragon and chives.

FRENCH ONION SOUP MIX: dry soup mix, flavoured with onion and spices.

FRUIT MINCE (mince meat): we used a product containing sugar, vine fruits, apples, suet, citrus peel, rice flour, glucose syrup, food acids, spices, salt and roast malt extract.

GARAM MASALA: often used in Indian cooking, this spice combines cardamom, cinnamon, cloves, coriander, cumin and nutmeg in varying proportions. Sometimes pepper is used to make a hot variation.

GHERKIN: cornichon.

GLUCOSE SYRUP (liquid glucose): a clear, thick syrup made from wheat starch.

GOLDEN SYRUP: a golden-coloured syrup made from sugar cane. Maple syrup, pancake syrup or honey can be substituted.

GRAND MARNIER: an orange-flavoured liqueur.

GRAVLAX: marinated, uncooked salmon.

GREEN SHALLOTS: also known as scallions, eschalots and green onions. Do not confuse with the small golden shallots.

HERBS:

KUMARA: orange-coloured sweet potato.

LEMON BUTTER: lemon curd or lemon cheese.

LEMON GRASS: available from Asian food stores.

LEMON PEPPER: a blend of crushed black pepper, lemon, herbs and spices; it is used as a seasoning.

LETTUCE:

Butter: a type of lettuce with soft-textured leaves and a delicate flavour.

Radicchio: a type of Italian lettuce with dark burgundy leaves.

LUMPFISH ROE CAVIAR: a cheaper substitute for caviar.

MUSHROOMS:

Button: small, unopened mushrooms with a delicate flavour.

Dried Chinese: unique in flavour.

Enoki: also called golden mushrooms; usually sold joined in a clump. They are tiny mushrooms with a small round head on a thin stem, mild in flavour with a crisp texture.

Flat: large, soft, flat mushrooms with a rich earthy flavour.

Shiitake: used mainly in Chinese and Japanese cooking.

Swiss brown: light to dark brown mushrooms with full-bodied flavour.

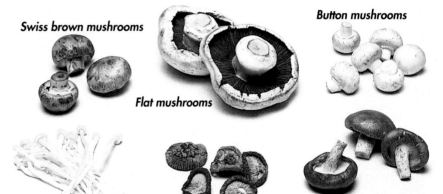

Swiss brown mushrooms
Flat mushrooms
Button mushrooms
Enoki mushrooms
Chinese dried mushrooms
Shiitake mushrooms

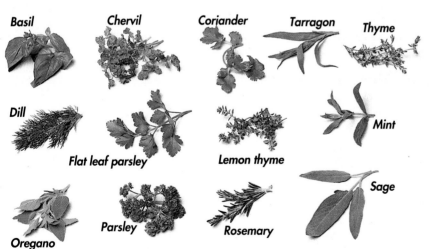

Basil
Chervil
Coriander
Tarragon
Thyme
Dill
Flat leaf parsley
Lemon thyme
Mint
Oregano
Parsley
Rosemary
Sage

HUMMUS: a paste of chickpeas, tahini, garlic, lemon juice and olive oil.

ITALIAN SAUSAGES: small, fresh, lightly salted pork sausages.

JALAPENO PEPPERS: hot chillies, available in brine in bottles and cans.

JAM (conserve): a preserve of sugar and fruit.

KAHLUA: a coffee-flavoured liqueur.

KIRSCH: a cherry-flavoured liqueur.

KIWI FRUIT: also known as Chinese gooseberry.

MACADAMIAS: Queensland or Hawaiian nuts.

MALIBU: a coconut-flavoured rum.

MAPLE SYRUP: we used a good-quality imported maple syrup.

MARZIPAN: is made from sugar, almonds and liquid glucose. We used a product available in 200g packets.

MIRIN: sweet rice wine used in Japanese cooking.

MIXED PEEL: candied citrus peel.

OIL:

Light olive: a mild-flavoured olive oil.

Olive: a blend of refined and virgin olive oils, good for everyday cooking.

Peanut: made from ground peanuts, commonly used in Asian cooking; however, a lighter salad type of oil can be used.

Sesame: made from roasted crushed white sesame seeds, used for flavouring.

Vegetable: we used a polyunsaturated vegetable oil.

PAPRIKA: ground dried peppers; flavour varies from mild and sweet to considerably hotter, depending on the variety of pepper.

PASTRAMI: spicy smoked beef, ready to eat when bought.

PASTRY, READY ROLLED:

Butter puff: frozen sheets of puff pastry made from wheat flour, 23 per cent butter, salt, food acid and water.

Puff pastry: frozen sheets of puff pastry made from wheat flour, vegetable margarine, salt, food acid and water.

Shortcrust: frozen sheets of shortcrust pastry made from wheat flour, vegetable margarine, glycerine, food acid and water.

PEPITAS: dried pumpkin seed kernels.

PEPPERS: capsicum or bell peppers.

PIMIENTOS: canned or bottled peppers.

PLAIN SWEET BISCUITS: cookies without icing.

PLUM SAUCE: a dipping sauce made from plums, sugar, chillies and spices.

POLENTA: usually made from ground corn (maize); similar to cornmeal but coarser and darker in colour. One can be substituted for the other, but results will be slightly different.

PRAWNS: shrimp.

PREPARED ICING: a soft white icing (similar to cooked fondant) made from sugar, glucose, vegetable shortening, gelatine and water.

PROSCIUTTO: uncooked, unsmoked, cured ham; ready to eat when bought.

PUFFED CORN: grains puffed under heat; a breakfast cereal.

RICE BUBBLES: crunchy puffed rice.

RIND: zest.

RUM, DARK: we used an underproof (not overproof) rum.

SAFFRON: available in strands or ground form; the quality varies greatly.

SAMBAL OELEK (also ulek or olek): a salty paste made from ground chillies.

SATAY SAUCE: a spicy sauce made from peanuts, soy sauce, ginger, chilli, onion, garlic, sugar and oil.

SEASONED PEPPER: a combination of black pepper, sugar and bell pepper.

SPINACH:

English: a soft-leaved vegetable, more delicate in taste than silverbeet; young silverbeet can be substituted.

Silverbeet: cook green leaves as required by recipes.

MAKE YOUR OWN STOCK

If you prefer to make your own stock, these recipes can be made up to 4 days ahead and stored, covered, in the refrigerator. Be sure to remove any fat from the surface after the cooled stock has been refrigerated overnight. If the stock is to be kept longer, it is best to freeze it in smaller quantities. Stock is also available in cans or tetra packs. Be aware of their salt content. Stock cubes or powder can be used. As a guide, 1 teaspoon of stock powder or 1 small crumbled stock cube mixed with 1 cup (250ml) water will give a fairly strong stock. Be aware of the salt and fat content of stock cubes and powders.

BEEF STOCK
2kg meaty beef bones
2 medium (300g) onions
2 sticks celery, chopped
2 medium (250g) carrots, chopped
3 bay leaves
2 teaspoons black peppercorns
5 litres (20 cups) water
3 litres (12 cups) water, extra

Place bones and unpeeled chopped onions in baking dish. Bake in hot oven about 1 hour or until bones and onions are well browned. Transfer bones and onions to large pan, add celery, carrots, bay leaves, peppercorns and water, simmer, uncovered, 3 hours. Add extra water, simmer, uncovered, further 1 hour; strain.

FISH STOCK
1.5kg fish bones
3 litres (12 cups) water
1 medium (150g) onion, chopped
2 sticks celery, chopped
2 bay leaves
1 teaspoon black peppercorns

Combine all ingredients in large pan, simmer, uncovered, 20 minutes; strain.

CHICKEN STOCK
2kg chicken bones
2 medium (300g) onions, chopped
2 sticks celery, chopped
2 medium (250g) carrots, chopped
3 bay leaves
2 teaspoons black peppercorns
5 litres (20 cups) water

Combine all ingredients in large pan, simmer, uncovered, 2 hours; strain.

VEGETABLE STOCK
2 large (360g) carrots, chopped
2 large (360g) parsnips, chopped
4 medium (600g) onions, chopped
12 sticks celery, chopped
4 bay leaves
2 teaspoons black peppercorns
6 litres (24 cups) water

Combine all ingredients in large pan, simmer, uncovered, 1 hour; strain.

All stock recipes make about 2.5 litres (10 cups).

Silverbeet

English spinach

SUGAR: we used coarse granulated table sugar, also known as crystal sugar, unless otherwise specified.

Brown: a soft, fine granulated sugar containing molasses.

Caster: also known as superfine, it is a fine granulated table sugar.

Icing: also known as confectioners' sugar or powdered sugar. Icing sugar mixture contains cornflour; use pure icing sugar, if specified.

SULTANAS: golden raisins.

SUSHI NORI: dried sheets of roasted seaweed. We used 19cm x 21cm sheets.

SWEETENED CONDENSED MILK: we used canned milk with 60 per cent of the water removed and remaining milk sweetened with sugar.

TABASCO: a sauce made from vinegar, hot red peppers and salt.

TACO SEASONING MIX: made of cornflour, spices, chilli, salt and pepper.

TAHINI: a paste made from crushed sesame seeds.

TAMARILLOS: an oval fruit with burgundy skin and tangy edible seeds.

TOFU (bean curd): made from boiled, crushed soya beans; we used firm tofu. Buy tofu as fresh as possible; keep any leftover tofu under water in the refrigerator; change water daily.

TOMATO:

Pasta sauce, bottled: prepared sauce available from supermarkets.

Paste: a concentrated tomato puree used in flavouring soups, stews, sauces, etc.

Sauce: tomato ketchup.

VINEGAR: we used both white and brown malt vinegar.

Balsamic: originated in the province of Modena, Italy. Regional wine is specially processed, then aged in antique wooden casks to give a pungent flavour.

Brown malt: dark brown vinegar made from fermented malted barley and beech shavings.

Red wine: based on red wine.

Rice wine: a colourless, seasoned vinegar containing sugar and salt.

White: made from spirit of cane sugar.

White wine: based on white wine.

WASABI: powdered green horseradish used in Japanese cooking. Substitute hot mustard powder or fresh, grated horseradish.

WATER CHESTNUTS: small, white, crisp bulbs with a brown skin. Canned water chestnuts are peeled and will keep for about a month in the refrigerator.

WORCESTERSHIRE SAUCE: spicy sauce served mainly with red meat.

YOGURT: we used plain, unflavoured yogurt with 3.4 per cent fat content.

ZUCCHINI: courgette.

Index

QUICK CONVERSION GUIDE

Wherever you live in the world you can use our recipes with the help of our easy-to-follow conversions for all your cooking needs. These conversions are approximate only. The difference between the exact and approximate conversions of liquid and dry measures amounts to only a teaspoon or two, and will not make any difference to your cooking results.

MEASURING EQUIPMENT

The difference between measuring cups internationally is minimal within 2 or 3 teaspoons' difference. (For the record, 1 Australian metric measuring cup will hold approximately 250ml.) The most accurate way of measuring dry ingredients is to weigh them. When measuring liquids use a clear glass or plastic jug with metric markings.

If you would like the measuring cups and spoons as used in our Test Kitchen, turn to page 128 for details and order coupon. In this book we use metric measuring cups and spoons approved by Standards Australia.

● a graduated set of four cups for measuring dry ingredients; the sizes are marked on the cups.
● a graduated set of four spoons for measuring dry and liquid ingredients; the amounts are marked on the spoons.
● 1 TEASPOON: 5ml.
● 1 TABLESPOON: 20ml.

NOTE: NZ, CANADA, USA AND UK ALL USE 15ml TABLESPOONS. ALL CUP AND SPOON MEASUREMENTS ARE LEVEL.

DRY MEASURES

METRIC	IMPERIAL
15g	½oz
30g	1oz
60g	2oz
90g	3oz
125g	4oz (¼lb)
155g	5oz
185g	6oz
220g	7oz
250g	8oz (½lb)
280g	9oz
315g	10oz
345g	11oz
375g	12oz (¾lb)
410g	13oz
440g	14oz
470g	15oz
500g	16oz (1lb)
750g	24oz (1½lb)
1kg	32oz (2lb)

LIQUID MEASURES

METRIC	IMPERIAL
30ml	1 fluid oz
60ml	2 fluid oz
100ml	3 fluid oz
125ml	4 fluid oz
150ml	5 fluid oz (¼ pint/1 gill)
190ml	6 fluid oz
250ml	8 fluid oz
300ml	10 fluid oz (½ pint)
500ml	16 fluid oz
600ml	20 fluid oz (1 pint)
1000ml (1 litre)	1¾ pints

WE USE LARGE EGGS WITH AN AVERAGE WEIGHT OF 60g

HELPFUL MEASURES

METRIC	IMPERIAL
3mm	⅛in
6mm	¼in
1cm	½in
2cm	¾in
2.5cm	1in
5cm	2in
6cm	2½in
8cm	3in
10cm	4in
13cm	5in
15cm	6in
18cm	7in
20cm	8in
23cm	9in
25cm	10in
28cm	11in
30cm	12in (1ft)

HOW TO MEASURE

When using the graduated metric measuring cups, it is important to shake the dry ingredients loosely into the required cup. Do not tap the cup on the bench, or pack the ingredients into the cup unless otherwise directed. Level top of cup with knife. When using graduated metric measuring spoons, level top of spoon with knife. When measuring liquids in the jug, place jug on flat surface, check for accuracy at eye level.

OVEN TEMPERATURES

These oven temperatures are only a guide; we've given you the lower degree of heat. Always check the manufacturer's manual.

	C° (Celsius)	F° (Fahrenheit)	Gas Mark
Very slow	120	250	1
Slow	150	300	2
Moderately slow	160	325	3
Moderate	180 – 190	350 – 375	4
Moderately hot	200 – 210	400 – 425	5
Hot	220 – 230	450 – 475	6
Very hot	240 – 250	500 – 525	7

TWO GREAT OFFERS FROM THE AWW HOME LIBRARY

Here's the perfect way to keep your Home Library books in order, clean and within easy reach. More than a dozen books fit into this smart silver grey vinyl folder. PRICE: Australia $11.95; elsewhere $21.95; prices include postage and handling. To order your holder, see the details below.

All recipes in the AWW Home Library are created using Australia's unique system of metric cups and spoons. While it is relatively easy for overseas readers to make any minor conversions required, it is easier still to own this durable set of Australian cups and spoons (photographed). PRICE : Australia: $5.95; New Zealand: $A8.00; elsewhere: $A9.95; prices include postage & handling.
his offer is available in all countries.

TO ORDER YOUR METRIC MEASURING SET OR BOOK HOLDER:

PHONE: Have your credit card details ready. Sydney: (02) 260 0035; **elsewhere in Australia:** 008 252 515 (free call, Mon-Fri, 9am-5pm) or FAX your order to (02) 267 4363 or MAIL your order by photocopying or cutting out and completing the coupon below.

PAYMENT: **Australian residents:** We accept the credit cards listed, money orders and cheques. **Overseas residents:** We accept the credit cards listed, drafts in $A drawn on an Australian bank, also English, New Zealand and U.S. cheques in the currency of the country of issue.
Credit card charges are at the exchange rate current at the time of payment.

Please photocopy and complete coupon and fax or send to:
AWW Home Library Reader Offer, ACP Direct, PO Box 7036, Sydney 2001.